pretty little **potholders**

pretty little **potholders**

LARK

SENIOR EDITOR
Valerie Van Arsdale Shrader

PRODUCTION EDITOR
Nathalie Mornu

ART DIRECTOR
Megan Kirby

COVER DESIGNER
Carol Morse Barnao

EDITORIAL ASSISTANCE
Kathleen McCafferty

ILLUSTRATIONS
Susan McBride

TEMPLATES
Orrin Lundgren

PHOTOGRAPHER
Stewart O'Shields

An Imprint of Sterling Publishing
387 Park Avenue South
New York, NY 10016

First Paperback Edition 2013
© 2008, Lark Books, A Division of Sterling Publishing Co., Inc.

ISBN 13: 978-1-60059-200-3 (hardcover) 978-1-4547-0854-4 (paperback)

The Library of Congress has cataloged the hardcover edition as follows:
Pretty little potholders / Valerie Van Arsdale Shrader.
    p. cm.
Includes index.
ISBN-13: 978-1-60059-200-3 (hc-plc with jacket : alk. paper)
ISBN-10: 1-60059-200-7 (hc-plc with jacket : alk. paper)
1. Potholders. 2. Textile crafts. I. Title.
TT699.S535 2008
746--dc22

                                          2007041354

Distributed in Canada by Sterling Publishing
c/o Canadian Manda Group, 165 Dufferin Street
Toronto, Ontario, Canada M6K 3H6
Distributed in the United Kingdom by GMC Distribution Services
Castle Place, 166 High Street, Lewes, East Sussex, England BN7 1XU
Distributed in Australia by Capricorn Link (Australia) Pty. Ltd.
P.O. Box 704, Windsor, NSW 2756, Australia

For information about custom editions, special sales, and premium and corporate purchases, please contact Sterling Special Sales at 800-805-5489 or specialsales@sterlingpublishing.com.

Email academic@larkbooks.com for information about desk and examination copies. The complete policy can be found at larkcrafts.com.

Every effort has been made to ensure that all the information in this book is accurate. However, due to differing conditions, tools, and individual skills, the publisher cannot be responsible for any injuries, losses, and other damages that may result from the use of the information in this book.

Manufactured in China

2 4 6 8 10 9 7 5 3 1

larkcrafts.com

contents

introduction

We made them in camp, we tossed them in drawers, and we've even singed a few over the years—talk about trial by fire. But now they're back. Out of the drawers and out in the open. Potholders.

You probably never imagined you'd spend time thinking about potholders. All things domestic once seemed so dreary, and hot pads—well, they're just plain ordinary. Think again. We're not talking about those homely store-bought squares that take the fun out of functional. The potholders in this book are pretty and practical, but they're really miniature canvases for experimenting with yummy fabrics and cool-looking textile techniques.

We invited some of the most talented designers working in needlecrafts today to raid their fabric stashes and make something worth holding on to. The results are eye-catching, inspired, and a breeze to stitch up. From hot pads to mitts, trivets to pan handles, this collection includes 32 beautiful, whimsical—and yes, even useful—potholders to cook up some fun. We've got a host of imaginative designs using pretty cottons, luxurious velvet, and lustrous silks. Flirty prints receive sweet little touches like playful pockets, yo-yos, beads, ribbon trim, and rickrack. As if that weren't enough, you'll find the perfect solution for recycling old sweaters and table linens, discover a nifty way to showcase a beloved recipe, and learn all sorts of new ways to hang your potholders with pizzazz.

The projects contain a range of fun techniques, including appliqué, embroidery, quilting, and photo transfer, all of which you can use on any sewing project. There's a hot pad to embroider with pretty little desserts. A set of potholders made from a boring old beach towel gets jazzed up with bias tape you cut yourself from a colorful print fabric. The appliquéd wings of a mitt shaped like a butterfly double as pockets; slip your fingers inside to protect them from heat.

Bring these cool projects from the craft room into the kitchen, and you'll be ready to handle just about anything. Best of all, since potholders are small, they take no time at all to whip up. You can start a project after lunch and have it ready to show off by supper. After that, plates won't get dished up near the stove. No, no, no—these projects are so cute, you'll want to serve a steaming casserole at the dinner table, putting it down with a flourish and placing your new potholder beside it, just so.

And do yourself a favor—toss those ratty old singed potholders in the trash.

potholderbasics

*I*n this chapter, you'll get the background on the tools, materials, and techniques you need to make the projects in this book. For some this will be a quick refresher, but for others it's everything you need to know to "be in the sew," and you'll want to refer to these pages often. Either way, you should start by assembling your Basic Potholder Tool Kit (page 11). Most projects call for these items so, novice or not, you'll want to have them at hand.

Chances are, you already have many of the supplies listed, so dig through your desk drawers and crafts closets before hitting the stores. As you rummage, consider uses for your crafts cache. Making potholders is the perfect opportunity to get creative with your scrap fabrics and odds and ends.

potholder tools

SHARP SEWING SCISSORS

Sharp, quality scissors are an absolute necessity and the centerpiece of any sewing kit. Never use sewing scissors on paper as this will dull the blades quickly and make them useless on fabric.

Some projects may call for fine-tipped sewing scissors for cutting tight curves, detailed work, and fraying elements. These should also stay far, far away from paper, so don't leave them lying around in the kitchen drawer.

CRAFT SCISSORS

Craft scissors are ideal for paper, and you'll need some to cut out the pattern pieces from your project templates. Find a pair that feels good in your hand, with a comfortable grip and moderate length so you can make expert cuts on curves and corners.

PINKING SHEARS

Pinking shears have a serrated edge and leave a zigzag pattern that can help limit fraying. They can also be used for decorative cuts and edges, as in the Merry-Go-Round potholder on page 48.

BASIC POTHOLDER TOOL KIT

- Sharp sewing scissors (for fabric)
- Sharp fine-tipped scissors (for detailed work)
- Craft scissors (for paper)
- Measuring tape
- Ruler
- Straight pins
- Hand-sewing needles
- Thread
- Insulating material
- Scrap paper (for patterns)
- Pencil with an eraser
- Iron
- Sewing machine
- Water-soluble fabric marker

HAND-SEWING NEEDLES

A variety pack of needles should include everything you need for the projects in this book. Choose a finer needle for lightweight fabrics and a thicker, longer needle for thicker fabrics. Regular woven fabrics and silks do best with sharp pointed needles, and for some projects you'll need an embroidery needle for detailing.

NEEDLE THREADER

Can't get those renegade threads through your needle? Use this little tool. Put the wire loop through the needle, insert the thread, pull back, and voilà! Sew simple.

SEAM RIPPER

Think of the seam ripper as your true friend. We all make mistakes sometimes—stitch happens—but this friend won't judge or tell on you. It can steer you out of tight situations where scissors aren't able to tread and help you get back on track.

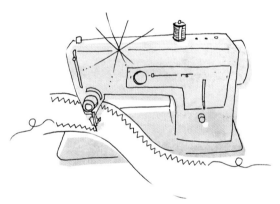

SEWING MACHINE

If you're the sort who prefers snail mail to e-mail and walking over driving, then you may take great pleasure in sewing these projects by hand, but for efficiency and speed a sewing machine can't be beat. For thicker fabrics, remember to use longer stitches and to reduce the pressure on the presser foot to allow the fabric to glide through the machine. For raw edges, use a zigzag stitch to keep the fabric from fraying.

SEWING MACHINE NEEDLES

Because it's easier to sew with sharp needles, be sure to keep extras on hand in case the one in your machine gets dull mid-project.

ROTARY CUTTER

If you've never used a rotary cutter before, visit your local fabric shop and try some on for size. Generally, the larger the rotary blade, the easier it is to slice through fabric. A good midsize cutter should do the trick and will work well for all the projects in this book.

IRON

For most, an iron is only good for getting wrinkles out of clothing, but to the clever crafter it's much, much more. Use it to apply iron transfers and appliqués and to press seams for patchwork and piecing projects.

SMALL FRY

For detailed work where your fingers need to get close to the iron, consider a mini iron.

Not only will this little helper get into tight spaces with ease, but it won't burn your digits when making bias tape or turning seam allowances under. You can find these small wonders in any craft store or fabric shop.

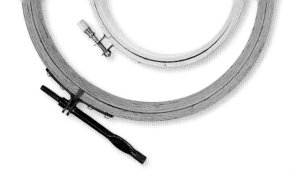

EMBROIDERY HOOPS

Hoops keep the fabric taut while you embroider, so it's much easier to do the stitching. They come in different sizes, but you won't need anything large for embellishing potholders.

PRACTICE SAFE CRAFT

If you want your potholders to be fetching and functional, you'll need to practice safe craft. That means choosing materials that won't catch on fire or melt when exposed to high temperatures. If in doubt, leave it out. Synthetic fabrics and embellishments like trims or dangling beads might not be the best choice for a potholder you want to use in extreme heat. Use common sense for each project, and take care to use enough insulation to protect yourself. It never hurts to err on the side of safety.

Always keep potholders away from hot burners and open flames. The only thing we want to ignite is your enthusiasm for creating these marvelous little works of art.

WATER-SOLUBLE FABRIC MARKER

For several projects in this book, you'll want to use a water-soluble fabric marker for embroidering, designing, and sewing. The ink will show up where you need it to, and should vanish with just plain water. But be careful—sometimes certain dyes in a material can make the marks difficult to remove, so always test your pen first on a scrap piece of fabric.

ON YOUR MARK

Completely remove any fabric pen marks with water before laundering or ironing to avoid brownish-looking marks that may set permanently.

potholdermaterials

THREAD

Buy a quality polyester thread for your machine and hand sewing to create strong seams that will hold up over time. Unless otherwise noted, use thread that matches the fabric for your potholder project.

FLOSS

Embroidery floss is a decorative thread that comes in six loosely twisted strands. It's available in cotton, silk, rayon, or other fibers and comes in every color of the rainbow. Although it can be time-consuming, (depending on the scope of the project), an embroidered element will transform your potholder from simple to simply spectacular and is well worth the effort.

FABRIC

Steer clear of synthetic fabrics. They burn more easily, and you don't want to get caught in a major meltdown. Cotton is always a safe choice and is used in most of the projects in this book. But don't limit yourself to fabric by the yard: tea towels and napkins are great choices, too, and have pre-finished seams so they're easy to use. Here's a brief description of the fabrics you'll encounter in the projects:

COTTON

Cotton is an obvious choice for crafts because it's durable, easy to sew, and comes in an endless array of colors and prints. With ample fillers, medium-weight cotton should work fine for most projects.

HEAVY CANVAS

Canvas is a heavy-duty fabric used for making sails, tents, and backpacks, and it's a great choice for potholders, where sturdiness is required. In the United States, canvas is graded by weight (ounces per square yard) and by number. The numbers run in reverse of the weight, so number 10 canvas is lighter than number 4.

LINEN

It's lustrous, strong, and durable (even stronger wet than dry in case your potholders take a dunk in the sink), and it comes in an array of wonderful colors and prints. Because linen is prone to wrinkling, it's best to press your fabric both before and after sewing to have a smooth surface for your finished potholder.

FAT QUARTERS

A fat quarter is a half-yard of fabric that has been cut in half so that each piece measures approximately 18 x 21 inches (45.7 x 53.3 cm). You've likely seen bundles of them in the quilting aisle of any fabric store. Size-wise, fat quarters are perfectly suited for potholders, and you'll use them in projects such as the Butterfly Flutter project on page 113 for both the binding and wing appliqué.

SILK

Who says silk doesn't belong in the kitchen? Silk adds a refined touch to even the most basic potholder. Choose a medium-weight silk that can stand up to some wear and tear, and use a sharp new needle when sewing. Silk also tends to ravel or fray easily, so seams should be finished. Check out Pretty Posh (page 94) and Lovely Lotus (87) for more silk inspiration.

CORDUROY

Corduroy is essentially a rigid form of velvet composed of tufted cords. Many projects in this book call for corduroy because it's durable, inexpensive, and pleasing to the touch. When pressing seams in corduroy, use a thick towel on your ironing board and keep the iron temperature on the lower side, especially if your corduroy is a stretch blend.

INSULATING MATERIALS

Most projects call for cotton batting, which is a safe, durable choice. As an insulator, cotton batting provides dense, even layering, and prevents heat build-up. It also won't melt from high heat, making it the natural choice for potholders.

Another good insulating option is the silver material you see on the cover of ironing boards, which is available by the yard at your local fabric store. It's usually made from 100% polyester that's been treated with a non-stick coating. Slip a layer on the inside of your project along with some batting, and you'll be ready to handle (almost) anything.

Needle-punched insulated lining also works well with cotton batting to reflect heat or cold back to the source. It consists of hollow polyester fibers needle-punched through a heat-reflective surface. It's important to note, however, that these materials are heat-resistant, *not* heatproof.

For other insulating materials, fleece and felt make good choices. Just remember that you may need to use more than one layer to make your potholder functional. The same is true for terry cloth. For extra protection, pair with a layer of batting for added insulation.

IRON-ON INTERFACING

You don't want your culinary experiments to flop, and your potholders or hot pads shouldn't flop either. Add support and structure to your project with iron-on interfacing. It's incredibly easy to use, but take caution: you won't want to use it on velvet or corduroy, as the iron will crush the nap. For these delicate fabrics, you'll want to sew on some non-woven interfacing instead.

potholder
embellishments

GETTING LOOPY

With potholders this beautiful, you'll want to display them where they can be fully appreciated. Adding a hanging tab or loop to your potholder will help ensure it doesn't get stuck in a drawer somewhere. Depending on the project, you may opt to stitch your tab to the front or the back of the potholder, or to baste it in between the front and back layers. Here are some materials you can use to make hanging tabs in a flash:

RICKRACK

Not only does rickrack add fanciful detail and creative edging to your potholder, but it makes a useful tab, as in the Girly Garden project on page 103.

ATTRACTION ACTION

If you're short on hooks, you can always sew small, powerful magnets into your potholders and stick them to the magnetic surfaces in your kitchen.

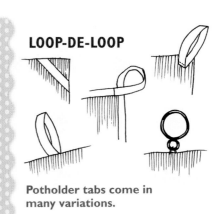

LOOP-DE-LOOP

Potholder tabs come in many variations.

RIBBON

As any true crafter knows, you can never have too much ribbon. Put some of yours to good use with a pretty loop to complement your potholder. See Retro Active on page 71 for more ideas.

JEWELRY CLASPS

Jewelry clasps such as round toggles add a touch of shine and sophistication to your project. They're also available in different shapes and sizes, so you can get exactly what you're looking for.

BIAS TAPE

You can easily turn the tail of the bias tape into a hanging loop. For instructions on how to make your own bias tape, turn to page 20.

DONUT BEADS

Stone, wood, shell, and metal varieties make striking tabs and don't cost much. Surf the web or visit your local bead shop for these round little gems.

DOLL COAT HANGERS

For Sweater Prep on page 36, the designer used a mini wire coat hanger as a clever hooking device. It's a look so cute that even Mommie Dearest would approve.

POCKETS

Pockets are always handy because they help protect your fingers. In Pompoms and Pearls on page 116, the pockets offer a way to store multiple potholders. In Butterfly Flutter on page 113, the pockets help create movement similar to a hand puppet. With a trick like that, you might even a score a little helper.

HOLDERS

One way to keep your trivets tidy is to make a fabric envelope to store them in. For the project Four-Course Meal (page 60), the designer created food-themed hot pads with a special holder.

basictechniques

CLIPPING CURVES AND CORNERS

When you sew a potholder inside out, all of the material in the seam allowance can bunch together when turned right side out. Getting rid of all that bulk doesn't have to pose a problem, however.

For fabric on a corner, before you turn the potholder right side out, clip straight across the seam allowance, halfway between the stitching and the corner of the fabric (figure 1).

For fabric on a curve, snip about two-thirds of the way into the seam allowance in several places (figure 2). This allows the fabric to overlap slightly where it was snipped and results in a smoother curve and seam on the right side.

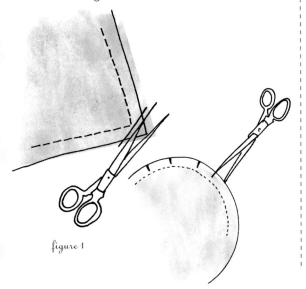

figure 1

figure 2

HOW TO SEW RICKRACK IN SEAMS

Add a splash of fun to pockets or to the edges of your potholder by sewing rickrack into the seam. The designer of Dot's Diner used this technique to add even more punch to a polka-dot print (page 34).

1 Position the rickrack on the right side of a piece of fabric so it is centered over the seam allowance. Pin the rickrack to hold it in place. Baste along the center of the rickrack (figure 3).

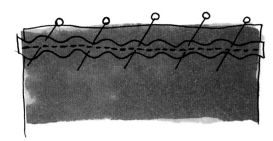

figure 3

2 Stitch the two pieces of fabric with right sides together. When you turn them right side out, the rickrack will be sandwiched between, with only half of it showing.

IN A BIND

Attaching bias tape (which is also known as "bias binding") might seem tricky at first, but if you follow these instructions you'll never get caught in a bind.

1 Measure the circumference of the potholder, add 5 inches (12.7 cm) and cut this length of binding strip. If you don't purchase double-fold bias tape, fold the strip in half and iron it. Pin the raw edge of the binding to the raw edge of the potholder. Stitch around the edge in the crease (see figure 4). Stop stitching 3 inches (7.6 cm) from the starting point. Clip the loose end so that 1 inch (2.5 cm) of tape overlaps the part that's stitched down.

2 Turn the bias tape to the other side, folding the long edge under, and pin in place. Slipstitch by hand to make an invisible seam (see figure 5), stopping 2 inches (5.1 cm) from the starting point. Alternatively, you can machine sew right along the edge of the tape, so the stitching hardly shows and catches the binding on the back (see figure 6).

3 To tidy up the ends, lap them by folding the loose tail under ½ inch (1.3 cm), as shown in figure 7. Finish stitching the binding down.

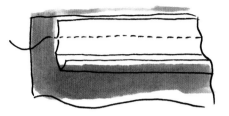

figure 4

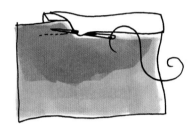

figure 5

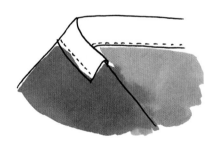

figure 6

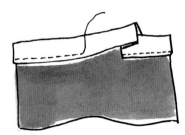

figure 7

HOW TO MAKE
YOUR OWN BIAS TAPE

Purchased bias tape is like a TV dinner—cheap and convenient, but ultimately pretty boring. For the perfect decorative finish, make your own bias tape. It only takes a few minutes and will make your potholder really pop.

1 Cut strips four times as wide as your desired tape at lines running 45° to the selvage (see figure 8). You need enough strips that, stitched together, will cover the circumference of the potholder plus some extra.

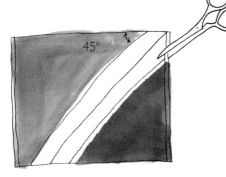

figure 8

2 Place one strip over the other at a right angle with the right sides together. Stitch diagonally from one corner to the next of the overlapping squares (see figure 9).

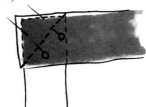

figure 9

3 Cut off the corners of each seam, leaving a 1/4-inch (0.6 cm) seam allowance (see figure 10). Open up the seams, and press the allowances flat. Fold the strip in half lengthwise right side out and press. Open the strip, and press the raw edges into the center. Now you have single-fold bias tape (see figure 11).

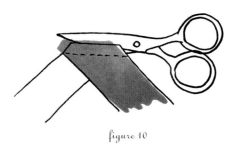

figure 10

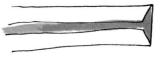

figure 11

4 To make double-fold bias tape, fold again in the center and press, as shown in figure 12.

figure 12

You can make your own bias tape in minutes with a bias tape maker. These handy gadgets fold fabric into perfect halves to create perfectly smooth bias tape in ¼ inch to 2-inch varieties, depending on the selected model. Simply pass your fabric through the tape maker, press and be impressed! You'll never have to worry about finding matching bias tape again.

figure 13

HOW TO MITER CORNERS

Mitered corners lend a crisp, polished appearance. Learn to master this technique in the projects Log In (page 68) and Lovely Lotus (page 87).

1 Stitch toward the corner, stopping ¼ inch (0.6 cm) from it. Fold the binding over itself, as shown in figure 13.

2 Fold the binding back down. Note that you've created a crease. Rotate the potholder 90° and, skipping the corner, begin stitching ¼ inch (0.6 cm) from it toward the next corner (see figure 14). Continue in this manner until you've stitched down all the binding.

3 Fold the binding over to the back side of your potholder, and fold the edges of corners by mitering (see figure 15). Splice the ends together, and hand stitch the binding to the front.

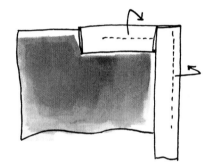

figure 14

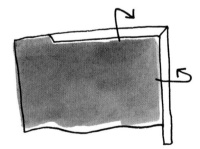

figure 15

HAND STITCHES

A few of the potholders in this book call for hand sewing in specific instances to mask the thread. If you don't mind seeing the stitching, however, go ahead and use your machine instead.

APPLIQUÉ STITCH

To camouflage the stitching holding on an appliqué, poke the needle through the base fabric and up through the appliqué, right next to the fold of the turned-under edge of the fabric. Bring the needle back down into the base fabric just a wee bit away. Repeat, as shown in figure 16.

figure 16

HIDDEN STITCH

Use the hidden stitch (figure 17) to close the openings you've left in seams to turn the potholders right side out.

figure 17

SLIPSTITCH

Slipstitch is another good stitch for closing up seams. Just slip the needle through one end of the open seam to anchor the thread, then take a small stitch through the fold and pull the needle through. In the other piece of fabric, insert the needle directly opposite the stitch you just made, and take a stitch through the fold. Repeat 'til nothing remains to stitch shut (figure 18).

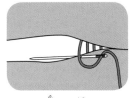

figure 18

EMBROIDERY

If you're new to embroidery, the following illustrations should help you master it in no time. Once you get the hang of it, you'll be hard-pressed to put it down. (Seriously, it's addictive.) Embroidering can be very relaxing, plus you can squeeze it in here and there. (Commercial breaks are a good time to get your stitch on!) Each stitch has its own unique function, and the overall look will transform your potholder into a refined little work of art.

BACKSTITCH

The backstitch can be used to create a seam or to outline shapes or text (figure 19).

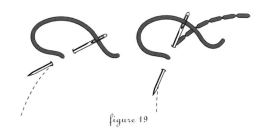

figure 19

BLANKET STITCH

The blanket stitch is a decorative and functional technique for accentuating an edge or attaching a cut shape to a layer of fabric (figure 20).

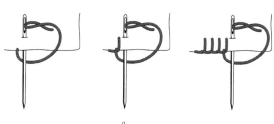

figure 20

CHAIN STITCH

The chain stitch, or "Lazy Daisy stitch," can be worked in a circle to form a flower (figure 21).

figure 21

FRENCH KNOT

This elegant knot is used to create decorative embellishment and texture (figure 22).

figure 22

RUNNING STITCH

This stitch is created by weaving the needle through the fabric at evenly spaced intervals (figure 23).

figure 23

SATIN STITCH

The satin stitch is composed of parallel rows of straight stitches, often to fill in an outline (figure 24).

figure 24

SEED STITCH

Use this stitch to fill in an outline with texture or color, like in Handle with Flair on page 55. Create it by randomly making small straight stitches, all the same length and facing in the same direction, surrounded by empty space (figure 25).

figure 25

SPLIT STITCH

Make a first stitch. For the second stitch, bring the needle up through the middle of the first stitch, splitting it. Then follow the line, with the needle coming up through the working thread and splitting it (figure 26).

figure 26

HOW TO MAKE YO-YOS

Yo-yos are little gathered rosettes that add a playful touch to your sewing projects. They are anything but tricky, take only minutes to make, and are totally adorable.

1 Decide how big you want the yo-yo to be, and cut out a circle that's twice as big with an additional ½ inch (1.3 cm) for the seam allowance.

2 Thread a needle with enough strong thread to sew around the circumference of the circle with some to spare.

3 Stitch around the entire perimeter of the circle, ¼ inch (0.6 cm) from the edge, folding the fabric under as you go (figure 27). Then gently pull the thread to gather the edges to the center, as shown in figure 28. Secure the gathered center with some stitches, and knot and trim the thread. Press flat with your hand, and you've got a yo-yo.

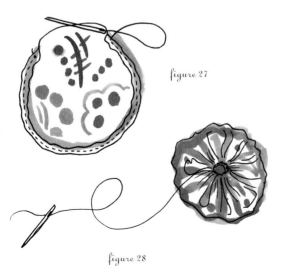

figure 27

figure 28

PIN TUCKING

A pin-tucking foot on your sewing machine can create decorative, raised lines in your fabric. The number of pattern lines and the spacing between the lines depends on the number of grooves in the foot. For a project such as Sew Romantic on page 108, a four- or five-groove pin-tucking foot works well to create narrow line patterns on the lightweight fabric.

PIECING

When sewing fabric squares together as in Kitchen Stitchin' (page 44), pin the first two squares together, right sides facing, then stitch along the edge using the desired seam allowance. Add more squares in the same way. When your row is complete, pin and sew the rows together.

QUILTING

Quilting is the process of sandwiching batting between two layers of fabric and stitching through all the layers to create a decorative, textured effect. Some projects in this book are quilted, and because of the small scale of potholders this can be done quickly and easily on any sewing machine. In the project Log In (page 68), you'll learn to create a log cabin quilt that's perfect for the first-time quilter.

GIVE US A HAND

You don't have to quilt on your sewing machine. In Recipe for Happiness (page 97), the designer quilted the house by hand.

BEADING

If you can sew, you can bead. Take your potholder from kitchen dud to kitchen diva by adding some sparkling beads. In Sweater Prep (page 36), beads are used to suggest buttons, and in The Bollywood (page 106) beads are added to embellish the print fabric. The result? Opulent, rich, and oh, so delicious.

USING PHOTO TRANSFER

Add a unique touch to your projects with personal photos or images transferred to fabric. All you need is your digital image, a printer, and some photo transfer paper to make it happen. Once you've got your image ready, print it on the photo transfer paper and then iron the transfer onto your project. It's that simple.

It only takes a few minutes but will help create a lasting impression. See Recipe for Happiness (page 97) and Kitchenette Silhouette (page 110) for inspiration on how to customize your pieces with this simple technique.

Here are a few helpful hints for transferring a photo onto fabric. Always read the manufacturer's instructions for your brand of photo transfer paper before you begin your project. Remember to flip the image before printing your photo on the transfer paper. Check your printer and image software settings for how to do this. If you don't flip the image, it will print backwards when ironed onto your fabric.

FUSIBLE WEB APPLIQUÉ

Several of the projects call for fusible web to create decorative appliqués. Here's the quick and easy way to master this technique.

1 Determine the size of your appliqué, and cut the desired amount of fusible web.

2 Iron the fusible web onto the wrong side of your fabric.

3 Draw or trace your template, and cut out your appliqué.

4 Peel away the paper backing, and apply your appliqué onto the background fabric.

I NEVER KNEW THAT'S HOW YOU FELT

Felting is the process of matting together wool fibers. It creates a wonderful thick material and is remarkably easy to do. Choose garments that are 100% wool, and remove zippers and buttons before you begin.

1 Put your washing machine on the hottest setting, add some detergent, and toss in the piece to be felted. Allow the washer to run completely through its cycle.

2 When the cycle is complete, check your sweater. It should shrink significantly. If the weave hasn't tightened enough, keep washing it until it does.

3 When the sweater is felted to your satisfaction, hang it up to dry. Don't put it in the dryer unless you want it to have a rough texture. Once it's completely dry, you can cut your felted sweater without it falling apart.

quick-n-easy

Even the simplest of potholders
can pack a visual punch.

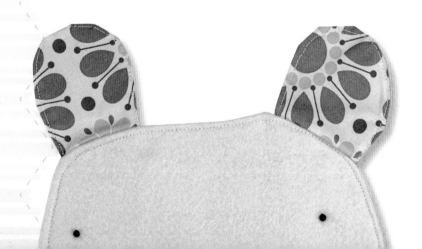

salsasofties

DESIGNER

NATHALIE MORNU

$\mathcal{G}$et your groove on in the kitchen with these terry cloth potholders that can also clean any spills. For added spice, make your own bias tape for the perfect decorative finish. It only takes a few minutes of effort and adds lots of zest to the finished product.

WHAT YOU NEED

Basic Potholder Tool Kit (page 11)

⅓ yard (30.5 cm) of fabric for bias tape

1 patterned terry cloth towel

WHAT YOU DO

1 To make enough bias tape for both potholders, cut four strips of fabric 2 inches (5.1 cm) wide, and sew them together sequentially to make one long strip. Iron them in half, and then in half again, as described on page 20. Set aside.

2 Cut two circles, each 8 inches (20.3 cm) in diameter, out of the towel.

3 Stack the circles together, matching all edges. Pin them, then stitch all around, ¼ inch (0.6 cm) from the edge. Trim a scant ⅛ inch (0.3 cm) all around.

4 Pin the bias tape all around the edge of one side of the stacked circles, lapping the ends with one turned under, as described on page 19. Stitch. Flip the tape to the other side, and hand stitch it down, using slipstitch.

5 To make the matching square potholder, enlarge and cut out the template on page 122. Use this as a pattern to cut two square pieces out of the towel, and repeat steps 3 and 4 with this pair.

VERY TERRY

Two stacked layers of toweling are thick enough that you don't need to insert insulating material between them.

mrs.rogers

$\mathcal{B}$e the first on your block to turn old sweaters and cardigans into funky four-square potholders. They'll have everyone asking, "Won't you be my neighbor?"

DESIGNER

BETSY COUZINS

WHAT YOU NEED

Basic Potholder Tool Kit (page 11)

Several all-wool sweaters or pieces of sweaters

Piece of cotton muslin, 8½ inches (21.6 cm) square

Piece of corduroy or other backing fabric, 8½ inches (21.6 cm) square

Piece of low-loft quilt batting, 8½ inches (21.6 cm) square

Washing machine

Rotary cutter

Self-healing cutting mat

WHAT YOU DO

1 Wash the sweaters on your washing machine's hot cycle, then air-dry them (see page 25). For a more felted feel, wash them twice.

2 After the sweaters are completely dry, cut four 4¼-inch (10.8 cm) squares, keeping the measurements accurate by using a ruler, rotary cutter, and cutting mat. Pin the squares to the muslin square in a checkerboard design, making sure all the edges are flush with each other.

3 With your sewing machine's zigzag feature, sew all four squares to the muslin base.

4 Pin the square of batting to the back of the square of backing material. Sew them together using a ⅛-inch (0.3 cm) seam allowance.

5 With right sides together, pin the back to the front. Sew, using a ¼-inch (0.6 cm) seam allowance, and leave an opening for turning.

6 Clip the corners on the diagonal, and trim the seams to eliminate bulk. Turn the potholder right side out and press well. Stitch the opening closed by hand.

REBUFF FLUFF

If you are "fulling" (making a piece of felt out of wool fabric) more than one sweater at a time, it helps to separate them in pillowcases with rubber bands securing the openings, to prevent lint build-up.

little bunny foo foo

DESIGNER

CHRISTINA ROMEO

*H*op to it! You'll love pulling all sorts of baked goodies out of the oven with this little felt-faced bunny in a funky patterned print.

figure 1

WHAT YOU NEED

Basic Potholder Tool Kit (page 11)

2 pieces of mustard-colored fabric, each 14 inches (35.6 cm) square

Off-white felt for the face

Patterned fabric, 12 inches (30.5 cm) square

2 small beads for eyes

Batting, 14 inches (35.6 cm) square

WHAT YOU DO

1 Place the mustard-colored fabric pieces together, and fold them in half lengthwise. Round the open corner, beginning the cut on the open side and ending it on the fold. When you open your folded pieces, you should have two identical pieces for the body.

2 Cut a large oval shape out of the felt; set aside. Measure a piece of the patterned fabric 5½ inches (14 cm) in height and a little wider than the body. Place this piece at the bottom of one of the body pieces, fold over its top edge, and sew it down with a straight stitch. Set aside.

3 To make the ears, cut out two 4-inch (10.2 cm) squares of patterned fabric and two 4-inch (10.2 cm) squares of mustard-colored fabric. Stack one piece of each fabric, right sides together, and cut out an ear shape. Repeat with the remaining squares to make the second ear, using the first as a guide for shaping. Trim the edges, turn the pieces inside out, press, and topstitch around the outside edges.

4 Pin the felt face to the upper part of the body, and topstitch it down with a straight or decorative stitch, sewing around the entire perimeter. Mark the placement of the eyes, and stitch the beads to those spots (figure 1). Sew or embroider a mouth.

5 Use the body of the potholder as a template, and cut a piece of batting. Place the batting on your work surface, then place the front of the potholder on it, face up. Pin the ears at the corners of the face, back sides up, matching raw edges. Pin the back to the front, right sides together, and match the edges.

6 Beginning at the center of the bottom edge, sew around the bunny shape, leaving an opening of 2 inches (5.1 cm). Trim the edges and then turn the potholder right side out. Fold the open edges to the inside and press. Close the potholder by sewing a simple straight stitch all the way around the exterior.

dot's diner

Who doesn't love polka dots? Even better, you can slip your hand in the secret pocket and hold a steaming hot dish in safe, sassy style.

DESIGNER

WENDI GRATZ

WHAT YOU NEED

Basic Potholder Tool Kit (page 11)

¼ yard (22.9 cm) of fabric

⅛ yard (11.4 cm) of fabric for bias tape

¼ yard (22.9 cm) of cotton batting

8 inches (20.3 cm) of rickrack ½ inch (1.3 cm) wide

SEAM ALLOWANCE

¼ inch (0.6 cm)

WHAT YOU DO

1 Copy the templates on page 121. Cut two pieces of fabric from each pattern piece, and cut one piece of batting using the larger pattern piece, which serves as the front and back of the potholder.

2 Pin the rickrack to the front of one of the pockets (the smaller fabric pieces), ½ inch (1.3 cm) from the edge of the straight side and stitch.

3 Pin the pocket pieces right sides together. Sew on the stitching line created in step 2 with the rickrack embedded between. Open the seam and press. The rickrack should peek up from the seam.

4 Put the front piece face down on your work surface. Place the batting over it and then the back piece, face up. Finally, put the pocket on top, matching all the curved edges. Pin the layers together.

5 Make a strip of bias tape 2¼ inches (5.7 cm) wide and 40 inches (101.6 cm) long (see page 20). Fold it in half the long way and press.

6 Starting from the square corner, pin the bias tape along the edge of the potholder with the raw edges together. Stitch slowly around the curves to ease the fabric in, and when you get back to the corner where you started, stop the machine, and leave the potholder where it is. Turn under the binding at the beginning to the back of the potholder, and continue stitching about 4 inches (10.2 cm) past the edge of the potholder. Remove the potholder from the sewing machine.

7 Turn the binding to the back of the potholder. Hand stitch the folded edge of the binding to the back of the potholder. Stitch the extra tail of binding to itself so the raw edges are enclosed. Turn the tail into a hanging loop, and stitch the end securely to the potholder.

TRIM AND TIDY

As you sew, guide the raw edge of the fabric along the ½-inch (1.3 cm) mark on the throat plate of the machine so the rickrack passes under the needle. This will prevent the trim from shifting between the layers of fabric later and gives you a sewing line so the rickrack is perfectly embedded in the seam.

sweaterprep

&

verything's cuter in miniature, and this preppy little sweater is no exception. A doll hanger tops this potholder and acts as a clever hook.

DESIGNER

JOAN K. MORRIS

WHAT YOU NEED

Basic Potholder Tool Kit (page 11)

Pattern

Striped sweater with band at the bottom

Matching thread

12 inches (30.5 cm) of grosgrain ribbon, ⅜ inch (1 cm) wide

3 pieces of white felt, ⅜ x 8 inches (1 x 20.3 cm)

Wire hanger or doll hanger

Wire cutters

Pliers

White spray paint

5 glass buttons

WHAT YOU DO

1 On scrap paper, draw out your sweater design about 8 x 7 inches (20.3 x 17.8 cm). Draw the neckline straight across. Cut the shape out from the pattern. Place the pattern at the bottom edge of the sweater, and pin it in place. Make sure the sweater's two layers are even.

2 Cut the sweater shape out. On the front piece, cut a scoop neckline, and on the back piece cut just around the neckline a little. Save the rest of the sweater. From the lower edge of the sweater, cut off two pieces, each 1 x 5 inches (2.5 x 12.7 cm).

3 With right sides together, place the cut piece of sweater along the neckline with the raw edges up, and pin in place. Sew ½ inch (1.3 cm) in from the raw edge using a small stitch. Zigzag the raw edges. Repeat for the back of the sweater as well.

4 Place the grosgrain ribbon in place along the front of the sweater and pin. Machine stitch close to both edges.

5 Using the pattern, cut out the pieces of felt. Place the wrong side of the sweater on the piled felt pieces. Machine baste close to the edge all the way around.

6 Place and pin the front of the sweater, right sides together, with the back. Machine stitch ½ inch (1.3 cm) in from the edge of the neckline to the bottom edge on both sides, and leave the neck and bottom open. Zigzag the seams.

7 Machine stitch two rows where the arms would be with a small zigzag stitch.

8 Use a doll hanger, or custom make one using an old wire hanger. To make a hanger, cut the top piece to about 2½ inches (6.4 cm) long with the wire cut-ters, and bend it with the pliers into a small hanger shape. Cut each side piece to 3 inches (7.6 cm), and bend the ends into a circle. Spray paint the hanger white, or cover it with a ribbon.

9 Place the hanger in the neck, and hand stitch it in place. Be sure to stitch around the edges so the hanger stays in place. Hand stitch the buttons in place on the ribbon.

NO LOOSE ENDS

For best results, use a tightly knit sweater that won't unravel easily.

frayed and fabulous

$\mathcal{C}$reate a velvety chenille effect with winks of layered color. This couldn't be easier to achieve—just stack, stitch, snip, and run it through the washer and dryer.

DESIGNERS

ELEANORE BOCKHEIM AND LIESL GIBSON

WHAT YOU NEED

Basic Potholder Tool Kit (page 11)

Batting, 1/4 yard (22.9 cm)

1/4 yard (22.9 cm) of printed fabric

4 fat quarters (see page 16) or 1/4 yard (22.9 cm) of solid-colored fabrics

Walking foot (optional)

Quilting template plastic

Embroidery scissors

Bodkin or other tool for turning narrow fabric tubes

Washing machine

WHAT YOU DO

1 Cut one piece of batting 7 inches (17.8 cm) square, and cut two squares of the same size from the printed fabric. Cut a square that's the same size out of each of the solid-colored fabrics.

2 On your work surface, place a square of printed fabric, right side down. On top of it, layer the batting then the four solid-colored squares in alternating colors. Top the stack with the remaining square of printed fabric, right side up. Pin or baste the layers together.

3 With a ruler and chalk or disappearing ink, draw a diagonal line from corner to corner on the top fabric, creating an X. Stitch the lines of the X.

4 Starting with one quadrant of the X, sew a series of parallel lines, each ⅜ inch (1 cm) apart. To do so, start at the outside edge of the potholder, and when you reach the original X stitching, pivot and stitch beside the original diagonal line for a distance of ⅜ inch (1 cm). Pivot again, and sew another parallel line back out toward the edge of the potholder (figure 1).

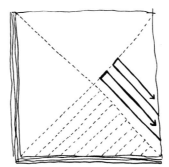

figure 1

5 Continue stitching parallel rows this way until you have filled the first quadrant with channels, each stitched ⅜ inch (1 cm) from each other. Fill the other quadrants in the same way.

6 Cut a narrow strip of quilting template plastic, about ¼ x 6 inches (0.6 x 15.2 cm). Round the ends of the strip. Slide the plastic into one stitched channel, slipping it under the fourth layer of fabric, to protect the bottom layer beneath. Cut through the upper layers of fabric along the center of the channel (figure 2); stop snipping right before you reach the stitched lines of the X. Remove the plastic strip, and insert it into the next channel, repeating the process. Cut each of the channels in this manner.

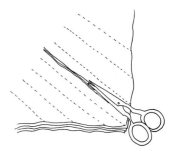

figure 2

JUMP IN THE FRAY

Don't pre-wash the fabrics before sewing: that way, they'll fray better in the last step. Select a printed fabric for the top, the back, and the binding, while using a variety of coordinating solid colors for the interior layers. This combination packs more visual punch.

7 Cut two strips of fabric (solid or printed), each 2½ inches (6.4 cm) wide and 18 inches (45.7 cm) long. Join the two strips, right sides together, along one end to form a single length, and use this strip as a binding to finish the raw edges of the potholder.

8 Cut a narrow strip of printed fabric, ¾ x 5 inches (1.9 x 12.7 cm). Fold this strip in half lengthwise, right sides together, and sew along the long edge using a ¼-inch (0.6 cm) seam allowance. Trim the seam, and turn the tube right side out. Fold the two ends under, and stitch them to the back of the potholder in one corner to form a hanging loop.

9 Machine wash and dry the potholder to fray the raw edges.

stitchingpretty

*E*mbroidered elements add zest to potholders. Spice up your projects with a dash of satin stitch or a splash of chain stitch.

tastys

kitchenstitchin'

DESIGNER

BETSY COUZINS

*Y*ou'll never forget to pick up the milk again—not with this nine-patch hot pad that elevates kitchen staples with simple embroidery.

WHAT YOU NEED

Basic Potholder Tool Kit (page 11)

Fat quarters of all-cotton fabric in 3 prints

Embroidery floss

Tapestry needle

Embroidery hoop

Rotary cutter

Self-healing cutting mat

Low-loft quilt batting

Extra-wide, double-fold bias tape

SEAM ALLOWANCE

1/4 inch (0.6 cm)

WHAT YOU DO

1 Transfer the embroidery template on page 121 onto one of the fabrics, leaving plenty of room around each design. Using the split stitch (see page 23), embroider each motif.

2 Iron the embroidered fabric. Draw four squares with sides 3 1/4 inches (8.3 cm) long around the motifs, centering the designs within them. Cut them out. Iron the two other fabrics, and cut out five more blocks with sides 3 1/4 inches (8.3 cm) long. Lay out the blocks in a checkerboard design.

3 Placing the right sides together, sew the squares of the top row. Press the seams to the side. Repeat for the two other rows. Again with right sides together, sew the top row to the middle row. In the same way, sew the middle row to the bottom row.

4 Cut a back 8 1/2 inches (21.6 cm) square from one of the fabrics. Cut a piece of batting 8 1/2 inches (21.6 cm) square. Place the backing fabric right-side down on the work surface. Place the batting on top of it. Put the nine-patch on top of the batting, right-side up, and pin all three layers together.

5 Cut four strips of bias tape about 9 1/2 inches (24.1 cm) long, and bind each edge (see page 19).

COPY RIGHT

Here's one method for transferring designs. Make a photocopy of the desired imagery, and tape the sheet of paper to a sunlit window. Tape the fabric to embroider over the photocopy, and trace each design lightly with a water-soluble marker.

sweettreat

Finally, a dessert without all the calories! Whip up this tasty treat with sweet cupcake embroidery and a strawberries-and-cream color palette.

DESIGNER

AIMEE RAY

WHAT YOU NEED

Basic Potholder Tool Kit (page 11)

6 x 6-inch (15.2 x 15.2 cm) corner piece of pink patterned fabric

8½-inch (21.6 cm) square of white cotton fabric

6 x 2-inch (15.2 x 5.1 cm) strip of pink cotton fabric

8½-inch (21.6 cm) square of pink patterned fabric

Embroidery floss in dark pink, pink, brown, cream, red, green, and white

Embroidery needle and hoop

7½-inch (19 cm) square of quilt batting or terry cloth

WHAT YOU DO

1 Using the template on page 122 as a pattern, cut a corner piece from the pink fabric. Iron the curved edge under ¼ inch (0.6 cm). Pin it face up on the white square, matching corners, and appliqué it on.

2 Transfer the cupcake designs from page 122 onto the white square of fabric. Embroider them using split stitch and satin stitch (see page 23). Embroider a scalloped design along the curved edge of the pink appliquéd fabric, and stitch a word you think describes dessert.

3 To make the hanging tab, fold the 6 x 2-inch (15.2 x 5.1 cm) strip of fabric lengthwise, right sides out, then lengthwise again with the edges inside. Sew along the edge.

4 Line up the embroidered square with the pink square, right sides facing, and pin them together. Place the hanging tab at the corner, and pin between both pieces of material. Fold to form a loop that rests on the fabric.

5 Sew around the edges using a ½-inch (1.3 cm) seam allowance. Leave 3 to 4 inches (7.6–10.2 cm) open.

6 Snip the fabric at the corners, and turn the potholder right side out. Slip the batting or terry cloth square inside, and smooth it flat.

7 Embroider a running stitch (see page 23) all around the potholder, ½ inch (1.3 cm) from the edge and through all the layers, hiding the knot in the floss on the inside of the potholder.

8 Sew up the opening using a hidden stitch (see page 22).

FEELING LOOPY

To make sure a hanging tab sewn into a seam has the proper orientation after you turn the potholder right side out, just remember this: match the raw edges of the potholder and of the strip.

queen anne's lace

$\mathcal{T}$he prettiest of all the wildflowers, the Queen Anne's lace on these pot-holders will take root in your kitchen and bloom year-round.

DESIGNER

SHANNON UDELL

WHAT YOU NEED

Basic Potholder Tool Kit (page 11)

8½ x 18-inch (21.6 x 45.7 cm) piece of light blue print

8½ x 22½-inch (21.6 x 57.2 cm) piece of dark blue solid

Batting

Yellow thread

SEAM ALLOWANCE

¼ inch (0.6 cm)

WHAT YOU DO

1 Cut two pieces 5¾ x 8½ inches (14.6 x 21.6 cm) out of both the print and the solid for piece A. Cut two pieces 3¼ x 8½ inches (8.3 x 21.6 cm) out of the print and the solid for piece B. Cut two pieces 1½ x 4½ inches (3.8 x 11.4 cm) from the solid fabric. And cut two pieces 8¼ x 8¼ inches (21 x 21 cm) from the batting.

2 Pair up each A piece with a B piece, with each A piece right side up and each B piece face down, and with the right edges lined up. Pin and sew the right-side edges together.

3 Lay out each A piece right side up and each B piece face down with the left edge lined up. Pin and sew the left side edges together. Press each new piece open toward the smaller rectangle.

4 Fold each of the 1½ x 4½-inch (3.8 x 11.4 cm) pieces lengthwise with the right side out and press. Fold the long edges in to the crease, press, and pin together with the rough edges folded in. Topstitch along the pinned edge. Fold the long tube in half so the rough edges meet, and pin to make the hanging loop.

5 Lay out one piece of the larger print face up. Lay the loop, rough edges up, on the solid fabric. Then lay one piece with the larger solid print face down over these pieces, so the large and small rectangles line up. Lay the batting over the top. Pin together, and be sure to catch the loop and leave a 4-inch (10.2 cm) space open along the long side of the short rectangle.

6 stitch around the square, leaving an opening. Clip the corners, and turn the potholders inside out. Press flat. Pin the opening closed.

7 Using a straight stitch, machine sew around the edge of the potholder a few times, keeping the lines a bit uneven for a loose look. Stitch along the seam between the two rectangles three times.

8 Enlarge the template on page 120, and pin it to the potholder as a guide for stitching the bloom. Machine stitch at least twice along the curved stems. On the stem, stitch with both dark and light thread. Use yellow thread to stitch the buds, using a medium, closely spaced zigzag stitch, and go over the same area two or three times.

HANG STRONG

Reinforce the hanging tab by stitching back and forth over the loop a couple of times.

stackin' napkin

Your mom always told you to use your napkin— and now you can in a whole new way. Rickrack and artful embroidery transform an ordinary table linen into an extraordinary potholder.

DESIGNER

REBEKA LAMBERT

WHAT YOU NEED

Basic Potholder Tool Kit (page 11)

Printed floral napkin

Embroidery hoop

Black embroidery floss

Embroidery needle

Rotary cutter

Cutting mat

8 x 8-inch (20.3 x 20.3 cm) piece of fusible fleece

1 yard (0.9 m) of jumbo black rickrack

5 inches (12.7 cm) of black ribbon

WHAT YOU DO

1 Place one quadrant of the napkin on the embroidery hoop, and embroider a few floral motifs to accent the design, using a simple backstitch (see page 22).

2 Fold the napkin in quarters, and cut a 9-inch (22.9 cm) square through all four layers using the rotary cutter and cutting mat. Make sure to center the square around the embroidered area. The embroidered square will be the front of the potholder.

3 On the wrong side of one of the cut squares—but not the embroidered piece—center and fuse the fusible fleece according to the manufacturer's instructions.

4 On the right side of the embroidered square, starting from the top left corner, pin the rickrack 1/8 inch (0.3 cm) away from the edge all the way around the square.

5 Make a loop with the black ribbon, and with the ends side by side, pin the ribbon at the top left corner where the rickrack starts and ends (figure 1).

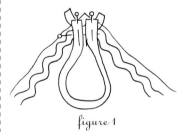

figure 1

6 With a sewing machine, sew the ribbon and rickrack onto the napkin 3/8-inch (1 cm) from the edge. Layer the four squares of napkin starting from the bottom with the embroidered piece (front) right side up, the piece with fleece backing right side down, and then the other two squares.

7 Flip the stack over so the back of the embroidered piece faces up. Stitch all the layers together 1/2 inch (1.3 cm) from the edge, starting about 3 inches (7.6 cm) from the bottom edge. Use the rickrack stitching line as a guide, and leave a 3-inch (7.6 cm) opening for turning.

8 To reduce the bulk at the corners, snip all four of them off (see page 18), making sure not to cut the stitching. Turn the potholder right side out. Push out the corners, and gently tug on the rickrack around the edges. Press out the wrinkles.

9 Slipstitch the opening closed on the back side of the potholder (see page 22).

GETTING CENTERED

Make sure the loop faces inward, toward the center, so that when you turn the potholder right side out, the loop is on the exterior.

merry-go-round

DESIGNER
AIMEE RAY

You can spin out these layered trivets in a variety of sizes. From coasters to hot pads, it's up to you which way to turn.

WHAT YOU NEED

Basic Potholder Tool Kit (page 11)

Patterned fabrics in different colors

White cotton fabric

Terry cloth

Pinking shears

Embroidery needle

Embroidery floss

WHAT YOU DO

1 Draw five circles of varying sizes onto different colors of fabric. Cut out each circle with the pinking shears.

2 Stack the circles face up, largest to smallest with the largest on the bottom, and pin them together.

3 Make a backing by cutting out a circle of white fabric that's a little smaller than the largest circle.

To make the insulating material, cut a circle of terry cloth that's a little smaller than the backing. Center the terry cloth underneath the bottom circle stacked in step 3, and place the backing beneath the terry cloth, as shown in figure 1.

figure 1

4 Starting at the center, stitch around the edge of each colored circle through all the layers.

EDGING IN

You can use a running stitch (see page 23) with embroidery floss in a contrasting color for a decorative stitch, or make tiny stitches with thread in the same color as the fabric if you want them to be hidden—or, use a combination of both.

handle
with *flair*

Slip these covers on the handles of your pots, and you'll get instant cred for keeping it cool. Make one or more in complementary colors, and hand embroider for added oomph.

DESIGNER

NATHALIE MORNU

WHAT YOU NEED

Basic Potholder Tool Kit (page 11)

12 x 12 inches (30.5 x 30.5 cm) of main fabric

8 x 5 inches (20.3 x 12.7 cm) of backing fabric

1/3 yard (30.5 cm) of fabric for making bias tape

8-inch (20.3 cm) embroidery hoop

Embroidery needle

1 skein of embroidery floss

1/4 yard (22.9 cm) of insulating material

WHAT YOU DO

1 Enlarge and cut out the template on page 119. Pin the template to the main fabric along the grain, and trace around it with the water-soluble pen. Remove the template.

2 Inside the traced line, lightly draw the design you wish to embroider onto the potholder. (Pressing heavily will cause the ink to wick across the fabric, resulting in a line that's not crisp.) Center the design in the embroidery hoop. With three strands of floss in the needle, embroider the entire design with seeding stitches (see page 23).

3 Leaving the fabric in the hoop, follow the manufacturer's instructions to cause the ink marks to disappear. Iron the embroidered design. (See the tip on page 56.)

4 Cut along the traced line of the template. Place the template along the grain of the backing fabric, trace it, and cut it out. Zigzag along the top edges of both pieces to prevent the fabric from fraying. Turn both pieces under along the fold line and press.

5 Cut two templates out of the insulating material, and trim away at the fold lines of each. Tuck one piece of insulating material into the fold of the main fabric, matching the lower, curved sides. Keep the

STITCH WHIZ

Embroidering the design will take a long time. You can speed things up by using fabric with an interesting printed pattern instead, and forego embroidering altogether. In that case, just skip steps 2 and 3.

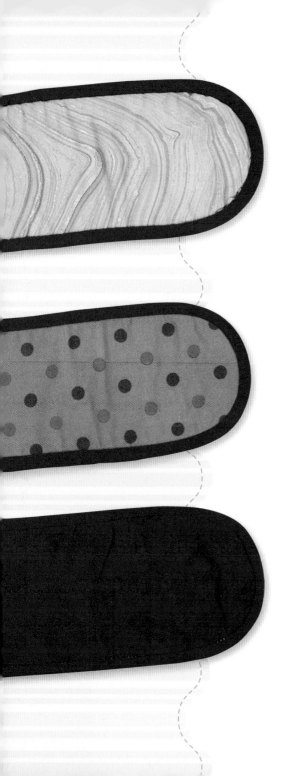

insulation in place by hand stitching along the top edge of the main fabric, sewing through all three layers, ⅛ inch (0.3 cm) from the edge of the fold. Repeat with the backing.

6 Cut a strip of bias tape 1 inch (2.5 cm) wide and 18 inches (45.7 cm) long, as explained on page 20. Pin it to the main fabric, working from the center of the curve toward either end. Turn under both ends of the bias tape then stitch. Press the seam from the front.

7 Stack the main fabric over the backing, with the insulated pieces facing each other and matching all edges. Pin to keep them in place, and hand sew through all the layers, stitching just on the outside of the seam holding the bias tape on. Flip the bias tape to the back side, and slipstitch it down (see page 22).

IRON, MAN

The most effective way to remove all the wrinkles on an embroidered project is to stretch the fabric as tautly as possible in the hoop, dampen it slightly, and slowly work a mini iron over and between all the embroidered areas.

scorchin'!

S ome like it hot, but your hands will thank you for making this protective, heat-resistant oven mitt. Batting material or terry cloth fabric provide the necessary insulation to keep you feeling cool.

DESIGNER

AIMEE RAY

WHAT YOU NEED

Basic Potholder Tool Kit (page 11)

Red patterned fabric, about 15 x 12 inches (38.1 x 30.5 cm)

White cotton fabric, about 15 x 24 inches (38.1 x 61 cm)

Terry cloth or quilt batting, 15 x 16 inches (38.1 x 40.6 cm)

Embroidery floss in different colors

Embroidery needle and hoop

WHAT YOU DO

1 Enlarge the pattern on page 122 and cut it out. Cut one piece of the red fabric for the back, and cut three pieces of the white fabric—one for the front and two for the lining. Cut two

more mitt-shaped pieces ½ inch (1.3 cm) smaller than the pattern out of the insulation material.

2 Transfer the flame designs onto one of the white pieces of fabric. Cut a "cuff" from the red fabric to fit the opening, making it with a slightly curved edge. Iron the curved edge under ¼ inch (0.6 cm). Pin it in place at the bottom of the white piece, and stitch it on using the appliqué stitch (see page 21). Select a word you like (see tip box); embroider it and the flames using split stitch (see page 23).

3 To make the hanging strap, cut a 2 x 7-inch (5.1 x 17.8 cm) strip from the white fabric. Fold it lengthwise, right sides out, then lengthwise again with the edges inside. Sew along the edge.

4 Pin the embroidered piece to one of the linings, right sides facing and edges matching. Sew ¼ inch (0.6 cm) from the edge, leaving the straight edge open. Set aside. Repeat with the back piece and the remaining lining.

HOT STUFF

Maybe your potholder's not scorchin' or *caliente*... It could be *brûlant, n'est-ce pas?* Or *het*, if you're making Swedish meatballs. Serve pizza piping *caldo* from the oven for dinner, and eat the leftovers cold for breakfast. And apple strudel tastes best *heiß*.

5 Snip the fabric around the curves, and turn each piece right side out. Slide one of the insulating pieces inside each mitt section, and stitch up the openings with the hidden stitch.

6 Pin both halves of the mitt, right sides together, with edges matched. Pin the strap ends at the bottom corner to form a loop. Sew ¼ inch (0.6 cm) from the edges, leaving the straight edge open.

7 Snip the fabric around the curved edges, and turn the mitt right side out.

four-course meal

$\mathcal{T}$hese scrumptious trivets are the full package! With a veggie, a side, and a main course, be sure to leave room for dessert. Afterwards, they tuck inside a fabric envelope, so tidying up is a breeze.

DESIGNER

JENNIFER WALLIN

WHAT YOU NEED

Basic Potholder Tool Kit (page 11)

¼ yard (22.9 cm) linen fabric

7 small scraps, each 4 inches (10.2 cm) square, of printed cotton fabric in blue, gold, and beige

¼ yard (22.9 cm) all-cotton fabric in four coordinating prints in shades of blue and gold

Paper-backed fusible web

Liquid seam sealant (optional)

Tracing paper

Embroidery floss in blue, gold, and beige

Embroidery needle

¼ yard (22.9 cm) polyester insulating material

¼ yard (22.9 cm) cotton batting or felt

Chopstick

Dish towel 20 x 28 inches (50.8 x 71.1 cm)

Walking foot attachment (optional)

⅞ inch (2.2 cm) button to cover, or purchased button of the same size

WHAT YOU DO

FUSE APPLIQUÉS

1 From the linen fabric, cut four 8½-inch (21.6 cm) squares for the fronts. Set aside. Note: Save a scrap of fabric for the covered button.

2 Fuse the paper-backed fusible web to the back of small fabric scraps, following the manufacturer's directions.

3 Copy the templates on page 119 and cut them out, then pin them to the fabric scraps and cut out the shapes. Don't discard the templates—you'll use them again in a later step.

4 Using the manufacturer's instructions, adhere the appliqués to the lower right-hand corner of the right side of each square, leaving a 1½-inch (3.8 cm) margin between the appliqué and the bottom and side edges of the trivet front.

EMBROIDER

1 Pin the templates to the fused appliqués, lining up the shapes.

2 With three strands of beige embroidery floss, embroider along the dashed lines with a straight stitch through all the layers. Hide knots on the wrong side of the fabric. Tear away the paper pattern, and remove all paper remnants.

FRAYED NOT

The appliqués will be applied to the trivets with a raw edge, so the edges will not be turned under. To minimize fraying, use a liquid seam sealant on the edges of your cut food pieces. Allow the pieces to dry completely before going to the next step.

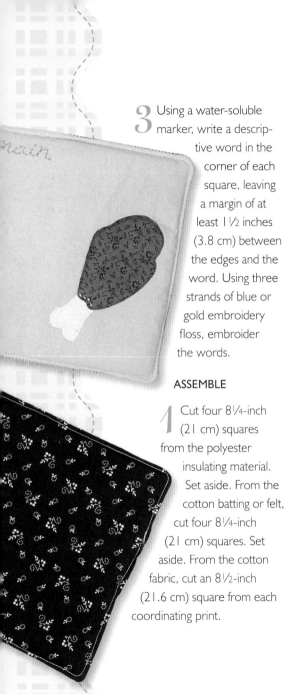

3 Using a water-soluble marker, write a descriptive word in the corner of each square, leaving a margin of at least 1½ inches (3.8 cm) between the edges and the word. Using three strands of blue or gold embroidery floss, embroider the words.

ASSEMBLE

1 Cut four 8¼-inch (21 cm) squares from the polyester insulating material. Set aside. From the cotton batting or felt, cut four 8¼-inch (21 cm) squares. Set aside. From the cotton fabric, cut an 8½-inch (21.6 cm) square from each coordinating print.

2 For each trivet, make a sandwich of four pieces in the following order: one back, right side up; one front, right side down; one square of polyester insulating material; one square of cotton batting or felt. Pin the pieces together, centering the polyester material and batting layers.

3 With a straight pin, mark a spot on each trivet 2 inches (5.1 cm) up from the right-hand corner of the sandwich for the starting point of the seam. Mark a spot 2½ inches (6.4 cm) above that as the stopping point. The space between the points will be left open for turning. Sew through all layers of each trivet using a ½-inch (1.3 cm) seam allowance, starting and stopping at the pins.

4 Trim the seams to ¼ inch (0.6 cm), and clip the corners (see page 18). Turn the trivets right side out, using a chopstick to push out the corners completely, and slipstitch the opening closed (see page 22).

5 Topstitch around each trivet about ¼ inch (0.6 cm) from the edge.

STITCH ENVELOPE

1 From the short edge of the dish towel, measure 11 inches (27.9 cm) along the length of the towel. Cut along this line to get a piece 20 x 11 inches (50.8 cm x 27.9 cm) long.

Fold in ¼ inch (0.6 cm) along the raw edge of the cut line, and press. Fold in another ¼ inch (0.6 cm), and pin in place. Sew along the folded hem to finish the edge of the towel holder.

2 Place the towel piece wrong side up with one of the shorter dimensions closest to you. Fold up the bottom 6½ inches (16.5 cm), and pin it in place. Sew along the pinned sides of the towel with a ¼-inch (0.6 cm) seam allowance.

3 On the back of the envelope, find the center point along the edge at 5¼ inches (13.3 cm). Measure ½ inch (1.3 cm) up from this point. Mark with a pin.

4 Make a buttonhole. For a ⅞-inch (2.2 cm) button, the buttonhole should be about ¹⁵⁄₁₆ inch (2.4 cm). The bottom of

the buttonhole will be at the point marked in the previous step.

5 To make a cover for the button, take a scrap of the linen fabric, and cut a circle 1 3/4 inches (4.4 cm) in diameter or the size recommended on the button package. Set aside. Using a water-soluble marker, draw flatware centered in the circle. Embroider the design with one strand of the blue embroidery floss, using a straight stitch.

6 Assemble the covered button following the manufacturer's instructions. Mark the placement of the button in relation to the buttonhole, and sew it onto the envelope.

TRAFFIC SIGNALS

It's helpful to use a straight pin with a green head as your start point and a pin with a red head as your stop point.

pretty piecing and cute quilting

Combine yummy fabrics with patchwork, then add terrific textures by quilting through all the layers.

now and zen

The fresh, clean lines and minimal design of this potholder may inspire you to ponder the meaning of life while you wait for your brownies to finish baking.

DESIGNER

MAITREYA DUNHAM

WHAT YOU NEED

Basic Potholder Tool Kit (page 11)

8 strips of coordinating fabric for the patchwork, each 4 x 1½ inches (10.2 x 3.8 cm)

Solid-colored fabric for the front, 5¼ x 8½ inches (13.3 x 21.6 cm)

Solid fabric for the back, 8½ inches (21.6 cm) square

Circular object—such as a bowl—to trace, 8½ inches (21.6 cm) in diameter

Piece of batting, 8½ inches (21.6 cm) square

2 feet (61 cm) of double-fold bias tape, ½ inch (1.3 cm) wide

SEAM ALLOWANCE

¼ inch (0.6 cm)

WHAT YOU DO

1 Design the patchwork section by arranging the strips, with long edges matching, to form a pleasing design. Stitch the strips together along the long edges. Press the seams open.

2 Sew the long side of the patchwork to the long side of the solid-colored front piece, right sides together, to make the top. Press open the seam.

3 Trace a circle on the top, centering it. (The entire circle should fit with a little extra space around the edges.) Align a ruler along each seam of the patchwork, and draw straight lines extending from the patchwork seam across the solid fabric.

4 Place the fabric for the back piece on your work surface, right side down. Stack the batting over it, and on top of that, place the patchwork piece right side up.

5 Pin all the layers together, close to the central line drawn in step 3. Machine stitch along the line. Remove the pins, and smooth the layers. Pin near the adjacent line, stitch, and repeat until all the lines have been stitched.

6 Cut around the traced circle. Pin the bias tape to both the top and bottom sides of the potholder, all around the raw edge. Once you've pinned around the entire circle, leave an additional loose tail of tape 9 inches (22.9 cm) long at the end, then cut off any extra material. (You'll use the tail later to create a loop for hanging the potholder.) Sew just the tail of tape closed, using a narrow zigzag stitch.

7 Create the loop by tucking the zigzagged end of the tail underneath the tape that's pinned around the circle. Use a zigzag stitch to fasten the bias tape all around the potholder.

IN STITCHES

Nothing says you have to use straight stitches to sew down bias tape. Most sewing machines have at least a few fancy stitches from which to choose. Use one of them to add another level of embellishment.

*log*in

*A*geometric wonder, the log cabin design of this quilted potholder is anything but square.

DESIGNER

BETSY COUZINS

WHAT YOU NEED

Basic Potholder Tool Kit (page 11)

Scraps of a variety of all-cotton fabrics, totaling about 1/4 yard (22.9 cm)

Piece of cotton fabric for the back, 9 inches (22.9 cm) square

Piece of low-loft quilt batting, 9 inches (22.9 cm) square

Rotary cutter

Self-healing cutting mat

SEAM ALLOWANCE
1/4 inch (0.6 cm)

WHAT YOU DO

1 With the rotary cutter and ruler on the cutting mat, cut the fabrics into strips 1 1/2 inches (3.8 cm) wide and of any length. Make sure some strips are at least 9 inches (22.9 cm) long.

2 Choose two strips for the center blocks. Cut one strip to make a 1 1/2-inch (3.8 cm) square. Leave the other strip the original length. With the right sides together, pin and sew on one side of the square.

3 Trim the long strip even with the square (figure 1). Press the seam open, then to the side. Choose the next strip of fabric, and place it right-side up on the work surface.

4 Placing the right sides together, pin the sewn pieces on top of the new strip, with three edges lined up and the extra length of the new strip continu-ing off to the right (figure 2). Sew along the top edge, and trim the extra length off. Open the seam, and press it to the side. Turn the foundation piece—what you've already sewn together—90°, so the newest piece is on the left side when facing up.

5 Choose another fabric strip, put it right-side up on the work surface, and repeat step 4.

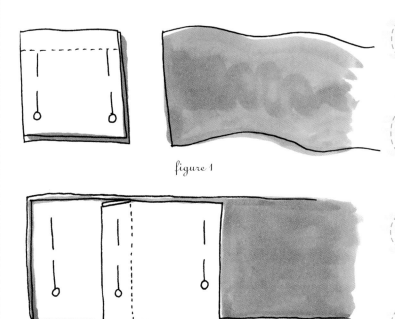

figure 1

figure 2

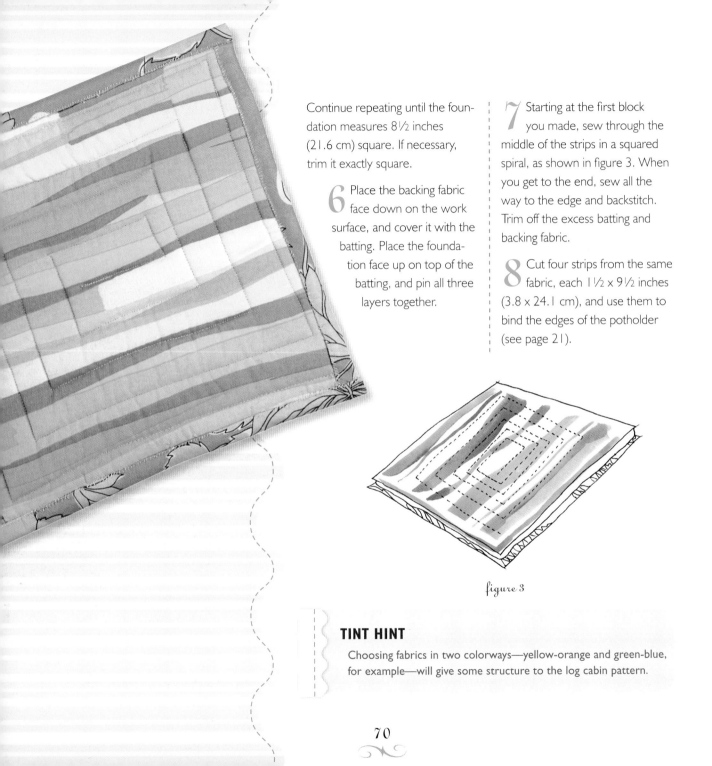

Continue repeating until the foundation measures 8½ inches (21.6 cm) square. If necessary, trim it exactly square.

6 Place the backing fabric face down on the work surface, and cover it with the batting. Place the foundation face up on top of the batting, and pin all three layers together.

7 Starting at the first block you made, sew through the middle of the strips in a squared spiral, as shown in figure 3. When you get to the end, sew all the way to the edge and backstitch. Trim off the excess batting and backing fabric.

8 Cut four strips from the same fabric, each 1½ x 9½ inches (3.8 x 24.1 cm), and use them to bind the edges of the potholder (see page 21).

figure 3

TINT HINT

Choosing fabrics in two colorways—yellow-orange and green-blue, for example—will give some structure to the log cabin pattern.

*retro*active

*T*he appeal of this retro little potholder comes from mixing a vintage tea towel with pretty, contemporary prints.

DESIGNER

SARAH MCDOUGALL

WHAT YOU NEED

Basic Potholder Tool Kit (page 11)

Fat quarter of each of four coordinating pieces of fabric

Piece of fabric from a vintage tea towel

Piece of number fabric

Pink thread

Sewing machine with straight and zigzag stitch

⅓ yard (30.5 cm) batting

6½-inch (16.5 cm) piece of ribbon, red or color of your choice

White thread

Rickrack

SWEET TWEET

Tea towels like this one sell for a song in antique stores and thrift shops.

WHAT YOU DO

1 Cut a piece of ribbon 6½ inches (16.5 cm) long, and a piece of rickrack also 6½ inches (16.5 cm) long. Prewash and iron all the fabrics, then cut them to the measurements in the chart below.

2 Sew the fabric's right sides together, starting with sewing the bird fabric to the bottom fabric. Then sew the side fabric to the fabric you just sewed. Sew the top fabric to the previously sewn fabrics. Press each seam with an iron after sewing.

3 Fold over all sides of the number fabric, and press to prevent fraying. Pin the pressed number to the front piece of the potholder. Using the pink thread, zigzag around the number fabric to fasten it down.

4 Place the top fabric of the potholder on the batting, and cut around the edges, leaving a ½-inch (1.3 cm) seam allowance.

Do this twice more so you'll have three layers of batting, and once again for the bottom fabric of the potholder.

5 With the top and bottom fabrics of the potholder right sides together, add the three layers of batting over top.

6 Fold the ribbon in half, and insert the folded edge between the fabric that's right sides together. Pin. Leave some of the ribbon's rough edge out to make the seam easier to sew.

7 Using the top layer of fabric as a guide, sew around three of the sides completely. On the fourth side, leave a 3-inch (7.6 cm) opening in the middle. Back tack the start and finish of each seam.

Top fabric	8 x 2 inches (20.3 x 5.1 cm)
Side fabric	3 x 7 inches (7.6 x 17.8 cm)
Bottom fabric	6½ x 2¾ inches (16.5 x 7 cm)
Bird fabric	4½ x 6½ inches (11.4 x 16.5 cm)
Number fabric	Cut out the number, leaving a ½-inch (1.3 cm) seam allowance around it

8 Trim excess batting and fabric on the three completely sewn sides. On the opening, leave about a ½ inch (1.3 cm) of batting and 1 inch (2.5 cm) of fabric, so it will be easier to close and hand-sew the seam. Turn inside out and press.

9 Tuck in the fabric opening and hand-sew. Machine sew the rickrack. Back tack both ends.

10 Quilt the potholder by sewing around the number and the birds, and add your own designs to make it unique.

EDGING IN

You can use a running stitch with embroidery floss in a contrasting color for a decorative stitch, or make tiny stitches with thread in the same color as the fabric if you want them to be hidden—or, use a combination of both.

nifty fifties

*T*hink June Cleaver with far more sass! This charming potholder and oven mitt set mixes '50s-style fabrics with cute, contemporary flair.

DESIGNER

AUTUM HALL

74

WHAT YOU NEED

Basic Potholder Tool Kit (page 11)

Up to 1/4 yard (22.9 cm) each of cotton fabric scraps in red and aqua or any combination

1/4 yard (22.9 cm) natural-colored linen fabric

1/4 yard (22.9 cm) fleece

12 x 20 inch (30.5 x 50.8 cm) piece of heavy canvas in a light color

4-inch (10.2 cm) square of red gingham

Rotary cutter

Cutting mat

White thread

Black embroidery floss

Embroidery needle

Seam ripper

Chopstick

Aqua button

Fusible tape (optional)

WHAT YOU DO

FOR THE POTHOLDER

1 Referring to the chart below, cut the fabric pieces.

2 Referring to figure 1 for placement, stitch pieces 1, 2, and 3 together sequentially. Press each seam open and then to the side with a 1/4-inch (0.6 cm) seam allowance. Stitch this strip to piece 4, and set aside.

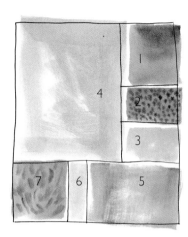

figure 1

Retro kitchen print	Piece #1: 4-inch (10.2 cm) square Piece #5: 4 x 5-inch (10.2 x 12.7 cm) rectangle
Red and white print	Piece #2: 4 x 2-inch (10.2 x 5.1 cm) Strap: 2 x 4 inches (5.1 x 10.2 cm)
Solid aqua	Pieces #3 and #6: each 4 x 2 inches (10.2 x 5.1 cm)
Blue and green floral	Piece #7: 4-inch (10.2 cm) square
Linen	Piece #4: 6½-inch (16.5 cm) square Back: 10-inch (25.4 cm) square
Red gingham	Yo-yo: circle 4 inches (10.2 cm) in diameter
Fleece	2 pieces, 10 x 10 inches (25.4 x 25.4 cm)

3 Stitch pieces 5, 6, and 7 together sequentially. After pressing each seam open and to one side, stitch this strip to the block made in step 2.

4 Copy the teapot design on page 123. Transfer it to the lower right-hand corner of the linen square using a temporary-ink marking pen or pencil. Embroider it, using a backstitch for the outline of the teapot and steam (see page 22). Satin stitch the heart.

5 Place the potholder top on top of the two layers of fleece. Use straight pins to hold it in place for machine quilting. With a long, straight machine stitch, topstitch close to the seam line on one side of each seam. Trim excess fleece from the edges, and square up if necessary.

6 To make the hanging tab from the 2 x 4-inch (5.1 x 10.2 cm) piece of fabric, fold the scrap in half the long way and press it. Then open and fold each long side in to the center and press. Fold in half to

enclose the raw edges, and stitch down the open side. Fold in half, and pin in place at the upper right corner, about a 1/2 inch (1.3 cm) in from the right edge.

7 Place the 10-inch (25.4 cm) linen square over the potholder top, right sides together. Pin in place around all four sides. Sew around all sides, and leave a place on one side for turning right side out 3 to 4 inches (7.6-10.2 cm).

8 Clip the corners, and turn right side out through the opening. Push out the corners with the chopstick. Press neatly, and pin the opening closed. Secure it with a hidden stitch (page 22).

9 Cut a 4-inch (10.2 cm) circle from the red gingham for a yo-yo. Make the yo-yo (see page 24), and stitch it to the corner of the potholder, sewing only through the front fabric and batting.

NOW YOU SEE IT...

By using disappearing ink, you can remove any marks not covered by the embroidery floss.

FOR THE MITT

1 Cut the fabric:

8 to 10 fabric scraps, 2 to 4 inches (5.1 to 10.2 cm) long x 4 inches (10.2 cm) wide

8 to 10 fabric scraps, various widths x 3 inches (7.6 cm) long for binding strip

Strip of red gingham, 2 x 20 inches (5.1 x 50.8 cm)

Strip for hang tab, 2 x 4 inches (5.1 x 10.2 cm)

Rectangle from linen, 6½ x 20 inches (16.5 x 50.8 cm)

Rectangle from fleece, 12 x 20 inches (30.5 x 50.8 cm)

Rectangle from canvas, 12 x 20 inches (30.5 x 50.8 cm)

2 Sew enough of the fabric strips together to make a piece about 20 inches (50.8 cm) long. Press seams to one side. Attach this patchwork strip to the gingham along one long side, and on the other long side attach the linen.

3 To make the binding (see page 20), sew strips together to create a patchwork piece 3 x 15 inches (7.6 x 38.1 cm).

Press the seams to one side, and fold it in half the long way, wrong sides together. Set aside. Make the hang tab. Set aside.

4 To prepare the patchwork for quilting, make a sandwich with the canvas on bottom, fleece in the center, and patchwork on top, right side up.

5 Machine-quilt with a long machine stitch in a random pattern. Fold the quilted fabric in half, right sides together, and be sure the seam between the linen and patchwork matches up. Cut out the oven mitt shape using the pattern. Stitch up the thumb side only to the top of the thumb. Open up, and pin the binding to the right side of the mitt along the bottom edge, raw edges together.

6 Stitch the binding to the mitt with a ⅜-inch (1 cm) seam allowance. Fold the binding around to the back and press. Pin in place to secure for stitching.

7 Stitch in place by stitching in the ditch, or stitching from the front side right at the seam line so the stitching is nearly invisible. Pin the hang tab in place on the open side near the bottom. Be sure to pin it so the raw edge of the tab is even with the raw edge of the mitt. Turn the right sides together, and finish stitching around the mitt.

8 Trim the seams, and clip to the seam line at the V between the thumb and hand section. Turn right side out, using the chopstick if needed to push the thumb out.

PRACTICE ATTACHMENT

Use a glue stick to hold the layers together for stitching. Apply glue to each layer, and press with a hot iron to set.

that's amore

 hat is love? To some, it's in the perfect meal. To others, it's in the details—like the small heart buttons, dainty stitching, and delicate patchwork of this oversize hot pad.

DESIGNER

KAREN WITTKOP

WHAT YOU NEED

Basic Potholder Tool Kit (page 11)

2 pieces of fabric for the front and the back, each 11 inches (27.9 cm) square

Medium-weight iron-on interfacing, 10½ inches (26.7 cm) square

2 different fabrics for the hills, each 7 x 9 inches (17.8 x 22.9 cm)

Fabric for the water, 11 x 3½ inches (27.9 x 8.9 cm)

5 x 11-inch (12.7 x 27.9 cm) piece of sheer tissue paper

Fabric for the bird, 3 x 4 inches (7.6 x 10.2 cm)

Fabric for the bird's wing, 2½ x 2 inches (6.4 x 5.1 cm)

2 scraps paperback fusible webbing, 3 x 4 inches (7.6 x 10.2 cm) for the bird and 2½ x 2 inches (6.4 x 5.1 cm) for the wing

Chalk pencil

Pinking shears

2 separated strands of black embroidery floss

Embroidery needle

6 small heart-shaped buttons in blue, green, and purple

Dense, thin cotton batting, 10½ inches (26.7 cm) square

6 inches (15.2 cm) of lavender rickrack

Black acrylic paint

Toothpick

SEAM ALLOWANCE

¼ inch (0.6 cm) except as otherwise noted

WHAT YOU DO

1 Cut all fabrics according to the materials list. Center and fuse the iron-on interfacing to the back of one of the squares; this will be the front.

2 Place the 7 x 9-inch (17.8 x 22.9 cm) pieces of fabric face up, and use the chalk pencil to draw free-form hill shapes on them, starting at the top corner and ending about 2 inches (5.1 cm) up from the opposite bottom corner. One piece should go left corner to right, and the other right corner to left. Cut along the lines with the pinking shears.

3 Pin the left-hand-side hill to the front, right side up, and topstitch along the pinked edge just below your cutting line. Repeat on the right side with the other hill.

4 Place the 11 x 3½-inch (27.9 x 8.9 cm) piece of fabric wrong side up, and draw a free-form scalloped edge for the water. Cut along the marked line with the pinking shears. Pin the water, right side up, over the hills at the bottom of the front and topstitch.

5 Using a water-soluble marker, sketch the word "Amore" in your best cursive.

With two strands of embroidery floss threaded in the needle, use a small, even running stitch, (page 23) to embroider it.

6 Fuse the paper-backed fusible webbing to the backs of the fabrics chosen for the bird and the wing. Copy the templates from

USABLE FUSIBLE

Follow the manufacturer's instructions in applying fusible materials.

page 118, pin them to the fabric, and cut them out.

7 Remove the backing of the fusible web from the bird and the wing, and place the pieces in position on the front. Iron to fuse them down. Slowly topstitch around the edges, using short stitches. Sew on the buttons in a design that appeals to you.

8 Place the batting on your work surface, and center the unembellished square for the back over it, right side up. Layer the front, wrong side up, on top of that, and pin all around. Stitch around the edges, leaving a 4-inch (10.2 cm) opening in one edge for turning. Clip the corners, trim any batting that extends past the stitch-ing, and turn right side out. Finger-press the project flat, and push out the corners. Neatly fold in the seam allowance in the opening, and press. Fold the rickrack in half, and insert the cut edges into the opening, centering it, to serve as the hanging loop. Pin in place.

9 Topstitch around the entire hot pad, 1/8 inch (0.3 cm) from the edge. To reinforce it, topstitch twice over the insertion spot for the rickrack.

10 Dip the toothpick in the black paint, and dab on the eye of the bird.

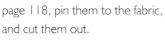

THINK PINK

Leaving a raw, pinked edge will allow the hills to fray a little bit when washed, which adds an appealing texture.

$\mathcal{L}a\mathcal{L}a$ voom

$\mathcal{L}$ike any true vixen, this oven mitt demands your full attention. So shake up some martinis, and pop in some appetizers. It's time to get glam!

DESIGNER

WENDI GRATZ

WHAT YOU NEED

Basic Potholder Tool Kit (page 11)

1/3 yard (30.5 cm) magenta velvet

1/3 yard (30.5 cm) cotton batting

1/3 yard (30.5 cm) cotton muslin

1/3 yard (30.5 cm) pink tissue lamé for lining

Magenta thread

Sewing machine with quilting guide

12 inches (30.5 cm) gemstone trim for bracelet

SEAM ALLOWANCE

1/2 inch (1.3 cm) except as otherwise noted

WHAT YOU DO

1. Cut two 11 x 17-inch (27.9 x 43.2 cm) rectangles of velvet, batting, and muslin. Layer the materials.

2. Mark two diagonal lines at right angles across the muslin. Stitch on the marked lines. Flip the layered fabrics over, and set the quilting guide to 1 inch (2.5 cm). Use the guide to quilt a 1-inch (2.5 cm) grid across the entire surface of the rectangle.

3. Enlarge the template on page 123, and cut two mirror-image oven mitt shapes and two lining pieces. Cut a strip of velvet 1½ x 6 inches (3.8 x 15.2 cm). Fold the strip in half the long way, with the right sides facing in. Stitch along the long side using a ¼-inch

(0.6 cm) seam allowance. Turn the tube right side out.

4. Pin the quilted fabric pieces together, velvet side in. Form a loop out of the tube you made, and tuck it into the seam allowance near the end of the mitt (see the tip below.)

5. Sew the mitt together, and catch the hanging loop in the stitching. Leave the opening for the hand open. Snip the seam allowance ½ inch (1.3 cm) apart around all the curves for smoother curves when the mitt is turned right side out.

6. Sew the lining pieces together, and leave the opening for the hand and a 4-inch (10.2 cm) opening in one of the sides.

7. Turn the quilted mitt right side out. Leave the lining inside out. Tuck the quilted mitt into the lining, and line up the opening for the hand so that the raw edges of "sandwich" and the lining is together. Pin. Sew all the way around the opening.

8. Pull the quilted mitt through the opening in the side of the lining. Leave the lining sticking out of the mitt. Hand sew the opening in the side of the lining, and tuck the lining into the mitt. Press flat the opening for the hand.

9. Pin the gemstone trim around the wrist area of the oven mitt. Stitch it down by hand.

FLIP TIP

The loop should be inside the mitt, so when the mitt is turned right side out the hanging loop ends up on the outside.

english breakfast

DESIGNER

LAURRAINE YUYAMA

*W*hen was the last time you hosted a real tea party? It's time to get dolled up and play hostess with this charming teapot-shaped trivet.

WHAT YOU NEED

Basic Potholder Tool Kit (page 11)

1/4 yard (22.9 cm) brown and red paisley print

1/8 yard (11.4 cm) natural linen with red polka dots

Scraps of plain natural linen

1/4 yard (22.9 cm) brown corduroy

Dark red ribbon

String

1/4 yard (22.9 cm) heat-resistant batting

1/4 yard (22.9 cm) polyester batting,

Thread

Embroidery needle

Brown permanent fabric marker

Safety pin

Wood bead, blue with red dots

Fabric glue

SEAM ALLOWANCE:

3/8 inch (1 cm)

WHAT YOU DO

CUT

1 Enlarge the templates on page 118, and use them as pattern pieces. Cut one front and one back of each, using the fabrics of your choice. Cut a piece of ribbon 8 1/2 inches (21.6 cm) long. Cut a piece of string 7 1/2 inches (19 cm) long.

2 Out of the heat-resistant batting, cut a rectangle 9 x 12 inches (22.9 x 30.5 cm), as well as one spout and a strip 3 x 8 inches (7.6 x 20.3 cm) for the handle. Trim off 3/8 inch (1 cm) all around the spout.

3 Using the polyester batting, cut a rectangle 9 x 12 inches (22.9 x 30.5 cm), one spout, and a strip 1 x 8 inches (2.5 x 20.3 cm) for the handle. Trim off 3/8 inch (1 cm) all around the spout.

ASSEMBLE

1 Pin together the pieces shaped like the tag on a tea bag. Place thread in the machine, and set the stitch length to 1.5. Topstitch along the sides and top, but leave the long side open. Trim the stitched seam to 1/8 inch (0.3 cm). Fold the string in half, and knot the end. Thread it onto the embroidery needle, and insert the string into the open end of the tag, poking the needle up through the center top (the knot should be inside the tag and catch on the topstitched seam). Sew the tag closed, and trim it to 1/8 inch (0.3 cm). Write the word "Tea" on both sides of the tag.

2 To make the front, stitch a lid to a pot, right sides together. Press. Tack the end of the tea tag string just above the seam. Center the ribbon over the seam, and stitch it down.

3 Make the back by stitching a lid to a pot, right sides together. Press. Stack both pieces of batting together, and pin the back to them. Trim the batting to the shape of the back.

6 Baste the handle, spout, and ribbon loop onto the right side of the teapot front, matching raw edges (figure 1). Place the back over them, face down, and the batting over that, matching all edges. Sew along the edge, leaving a large opening at the bottom. Turn right side out, and whipstitch the opening closed.

7 With the top of the trivet facing up, topstitch along the edges of the ribbon. Transfer the dotted lines from the pattern piece for the teapot bottom onto the fabric and topstitch. Press the handle and edges.

8 To make the hanging tab, cut a piece of ribbon 6 inches (15.2 cm) long. Stitch both raw ends to the top of the teapot. Thread the ribbon through the bead, and use a dab of fabric glue or a knot to keep the embellishment in place.

4 With the right sides together, lay the spout pieces on top of the heat-resistant batting over the polyester batting. Sew, leaving open the edge where the spout meets the teapot. Clip the corners, and turn right side out.

5 Sew the handle pieces together, right sides facing down, leaving the ends open. Turn it right side out. Roll the bigger strip of batting around the smaller strip and pin. Attach a safety pin to the rolled batting, and pull it through the tube.

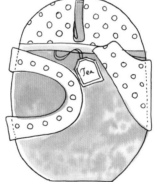

figure 1

ROLLIN', ROLLIN', ROLLIN'

To get the doubled ribbon through the hole of the bead, roll the tip of the loop and wrap it with tape. Poke the tape "needle" through the hole, pull the ribbon through, and carefully remove the tape.

 lovely lotus

𝒜 sacred symbol of beauty and purity, the lotus flower on this silk potholder achieves perfection and ensures luck in your most ambitious culinary endeavors.

DESIGNER

JOAN K. MORRIS

WHAT YOU NEED

Basic Potholder Tool Kit (page 11)

8 x 8-inch (20.3 x 20.3 cm) piece of white dupioni silk

¼ yard (22.9 cm) striped heavy cotton fabric

2 pieces of light-colored felt, each 8 x 8 inches (20.3 x 20.3 cm)

7 x 7-inch (17.8 x 17.8 cm) piece of gold dupioni silk

Iron-on adhesive

Matching white and gold thread

White chalk tailor's pencil

Flat pearl bead, ¾ inch (1.9 cm) in diameter and open in the center

WHAT YOU DO

1 Make a paper pattern 8 x 8 inches (20.3 x 20.3 cm). Using the pattern, cut out a piece of the white silk, a piece of the cotton, and two pieces of felt.

2 Following the manufacturer's instructions, iron the adhesive onto the back side of the gold silk. Copy the template of the lotus on page 120, and cut it out. Draw around the lotus design onto the paper backing of the adhesive on the back of the silk.

3 Cut the lotus design out of the gold silk. Peel off the paper backing, and place the lotus, face up, in position on the white silk. Iron, following the manufacturer's instructions.

4 Place the two felt pieces stacked under the white silk. Machine baste close to the edge all the way around. With the white chalk pencil, draw the petals onto the gold silk lotus. Machine sew over these lines three or four times side by side, and sew circles around the stamen.

5 Zigzag stitch around the outside of the lotus, catching the lotus and the background as you stitch. Cut an 8 x 8-inch (20.3 x 20.3 cm) piece of the striped fabric, and place it with the wrong side touching the felt and the right side facing out. The white silk with the lotus will be on one side and the stripe on the other. Machine baste around the edge.

6 Cut four strips of the remaining striped fabric on the bias, 2½ x 9 inches (6.4 x 22.9 cm). Place one strip right sides together

FAB TABS

When it comes to hanging mechanisms for your potholders, the sky's the limit. Hunt for old plastic jewelry with flat, pierced elements to dismantle. Stitch on a short, looped strand of shimmery beads. Look in the hardware store for rustproof washers. Bead stores stock tons of likely goodies: small cameo mountings look quite elegant, or the round half of a toggle might match your design perfectly.

with the silk side of the piece along one of the sides. Leave an equal amount hanging over the ends. Machine stitch the length of the side 1/2 inch (1.3 cm) in from the edge. Repeat with another strip on the opposite edge of the silk piece.

7 Fold and press these two pieces to the back of the potholder, and fold a 1/2-inch (1.3 cm) hem and press. This should cover the line of stitching. Hand stitch these two pieces down to the back side. Cut off the extra fabric at the ends, flush with the sides.

8 Machine stitch the other two strips, stitching right over the ends of the other two sewn-in pieces. Fold over the flaps at the end, and hand stitch in place. Press and fold over the two sides and the 1/2-inch (1.3 cm) hem, and hand stitch in place.

9 To echo quilt the potholder, stitch around the entire lotus design, 1/4 inch (0.6 cm) from its outline, then stitch again around the quilted outline, 1/4 inch (0.6 cm) from it. Repeat until you've covered all the white silk in quilting without stitching on the striped edge.

Hand stitch the bead to a corner to serve as a hang tab, using doubled thread wrapped around the bead five or six times.

DOGGED EFFORT

To stitch small, curved areas more easily, lower the feed dogs and use a darning foot if your machine has that feature.

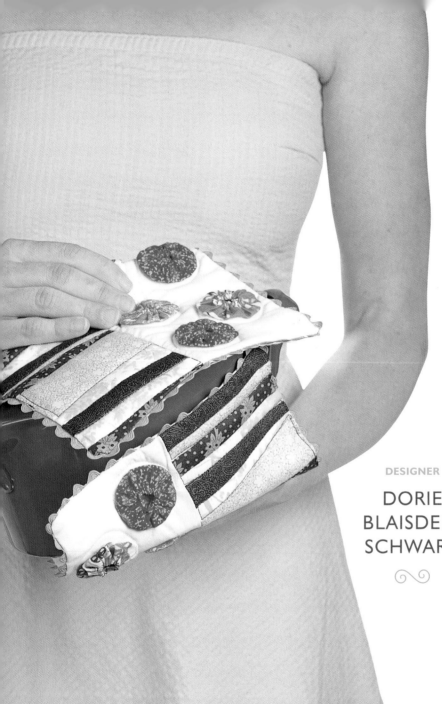

yo-yo*go*

*T*he best trick to this potholder embellished with yo-yos? After pulling a pie out of the oven, you can set it aside to cool and really go walk the dog.

DESIGNER

DORIE BLAISDELL SCHWARZ

WHAT YOU NEED

Basic Potholder Tool Kit (page 11)

¼ yard (22.9 cm) white cotton fabric

Green fabric scraps at least 5 inches (12.7 cm) long

Bright pink fabric scraps

Cup or another round object for tracing

Cotton batting, 7 x 14 inches (17.8 x 35.6 cm)

White thread

Medium turquoise rickrack

Green thread

SEAM ALLOWANCE

¼ inch (0.6 cm)

WHAT YOU DO

1 Cut one 7½-inch (19 cm) square of white cotton, then cut one 4 x 7½-inch (10.2 x 19 cm) rectangle of white cotton.

2 Cut the green scraps into strips about 5 inches (12.7 cm) long in varying widths, some at an angle.

3 Use a cup with a diameter of 3¼ inches (8.3 cm) to trace five circles on the wrong side of the pink fabric scraps, and cut out the circles. Cut two 6¾-inch (17.1 cm) squares of cotton batting.

4 To sew the grass, line up the green strips randomly, and arrange the angled strips to complement each other and make a straight line in the end. With white thread in the machine, stitch one green scrap to another, starting from one end.

When the sewn grass looks about 8 inches (20.3 cm) long, stop and press, pressing the seam allowance to the darker fabric where possible.

5 Trim the grass to 7½ x 4 inches (19 x 10.2 cm). Sew the white rectangle to the grass, and press the seam toward the grass.

6 Make yo-yos out of the pink circles (see page 24).

7 Pin the yo-yos to the potholder front. Evenly space three yo-yos directly above the grass, and stagger the other two in a row above. Sew the yo-yos to the fabric using a running stitch and catch just the back part of the yo-yo.

8 To assemble, pin the rickrack to the potholder front, matching edges. Then pin the back of the potholder to the front, right sides facing each other.

9 Stitch around the edge of the potholder, leaving a 3-inch (7.6 cm) opening. Clip the corners and turn. Slide the double layer of cotton batting into the opening. Smooth the batting, and stitch the opening closed.

10 Quilt the potholder by machine-stitching around the yo-yos and up and down the grass strips. To quilt on top of the green fabric, switch the thread color to green, but leave the bobbin white.

*fancy*this

Appliqué, photo transfer, ruching, and more—you won't find these cool embellishment techniques on store-bought potholders!

prettyposh

Y ou can feel like a queen, at least for a day, with the luxurious silk and pretty rose montage of this quilted oven mitt.

DESIGNER

JOAN K. MORRIS

WHAT YOU NEED

Basic Potholder Tool Kit (page 11)

1/4 yard (22.9 cm) light blue silk

1/4 yard (22.9 cm) blue linen

2 pieces of white felt, 7 x 9 inches (17.8 x 22.9 cm)

Piece of white felt, 6 x 7 inches (15.2 x 17.8 cm)

Scraps of hot pink, peach, and yellow silk

Piece of quilt batting 7 x 9 inches (17.8 x 22.9 cm)

Light pink thread

Blue thread

Darning foot (optional)

Hot pink thread

3/4-inch (1.9 cm) round silver toggle

SEAM ALLOWANCE

1/2 inch (1.3 cm)

WHAT YOU DO

1 Photocopy the template on page 121 twice, and cut around the exterior outline of both. Set one aside; this will be the template for both the top and back. To make the pattern for the pocket, cut along the horizontal line and discard the smaller piece of paper.

2 Using the top/back template, cut out a piece of the blue silk, a piece of the blue linen, a piece of the quilt batting, and two pieces of the felt. Layer to the wrong side of the blue linen piece a piece of felt, then quilt batting, then the other piece of felt. Machine baste close to the edge all the way around.

3 Place the blue silk right sides together with the blue linen stack. Machine stitch around the whole edge 1/2 inch (1.3 cm) in, and leave an opening 3 inches (7.6 cm) wide at the side edge. Clip curves (see page 18). Turn right side out and press flat, folding in the fabric at the opening. Hand stitch closed.

4 With the light pink thread, machine stitch a line from the left corner to the bottom right corner. Measure over 1 inch (2.5 cm), and stitch another line. Move over rows until you have the whole piece quilted. Then run rows of stitches from the right upper corner to the lower left corner the same way to create diamond shapes. Run another row of stitching over the first with the blue thread.

5 Using the pocket template, cut out a piece of the blue silk, a piece of blue linen, and a piece of felt. Machine baste the felt piece to the wrong side of the blue linen, stitching close to the edge all the way around.

6 Place the blue silk right sides together with the blue linen and felt piece. Machine stitch 1/2 inch (1.3 cm) in from the edge all the way around, and leave a 3-inch (7.6 cm) opening. Clip the curves. Turn right side out, and press flat. Fold and press the opening. Hand stitch the opening closed.

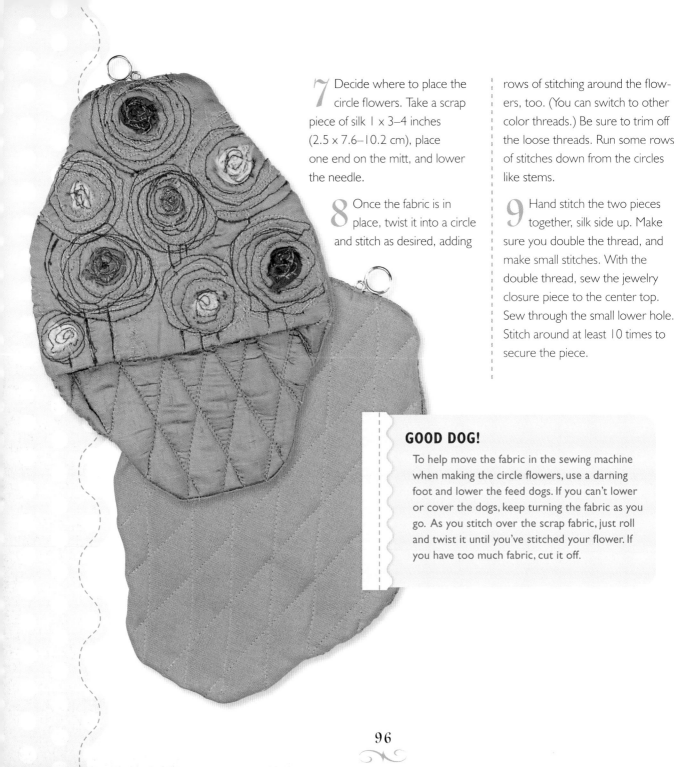

7 Decide where to place the circle flowers. Take a scrap piece of silk 1 x 3–4 inches (2.5 x 7.6–10.2 cm), place one end on the mitt, and lower the needle.

8 Once the fabric is in place, twist it into a circle and stitch as desired, adding rows of stitching around the flowers, too. (You can switch to other color threads.) Be sure to trim off the loose threads. Run some rows of stitches down from the circles like stems.

9 Hand stitch the two pieces together, silk side up. Make sure you double the thread, and make small stitches. With the double thread, sew the jewelry closure piece to the center top. Sew through the small lower hole. Stitch around at least 10 times to secure the piece.

GOOD DOG!

To help move the fabric in the sewing machine when making the circle flowers, use a darning foot and lower the feed dogs. If you can't lower or cover the dogs, keep turning the fabric as you go. As you stitch over the scrap fabric, just roll and twist it until you've stitched your flower. If you have too much fabric, cut it off.

recipe for happiness

*T*his little house has it all: one part yummy, two parts sweet, and a dollop of finger-licking fun. Use a treasured recipe that's been passed down through the years to create your own special keepsake.

DESIGNER

BETHANY MANN

WHAT YOU NEED

Basic Potholder Tool Kit (page 11)

8 x 10-inch (20.3 x 25.4 cm) washable, inkjet-ready, printable cotton sheet

2 fabric scraps in two main colors, 12 x 12 inches (30.5 x 30.5 cm)

2 accent pieces of fabric, 8 x 8 inches (20.3 x 20.3 cm)

Computer

Scanner

Inkjet printer

Rotary cutter

White thread

2 pieces of 10 x 10-inch (25.4 x 25.4 cm) batting

4 inches (10.2 cm) of bias tape

Large button

Thread in black or contrasting color to main fabric for hand quilting

Quilting needle

SEAM ALLOWANCE

1/4 inch (0.6 cm)

WHAT YOU DO

1 Choose a recipe card and a photo of someone enjoying the recipe. With the computer and scanner, scan and resize the recipe card to be about 2½ x 4¼ inches (6.4 x 10.8 cm) and the photo to be 2¾ x 4¼ inches (7 x 10.8 cm). Print the card and photo on the cotton sheet.

2 Follow the instructions on the package to set the ink.

3 Trim the photo and recipe card with a ¼-inch (0.6 cm) border on all sides. With the rotary cutter and ruler, cut

out the strips 1¼ inches (3.2 cm) wide for the front of the house. In a contrasting fabric color, cut out strips 1 inch (2.5 cm) wide for the roof. Then cut the striped window patch to be 2¼ x 3 inches (5.7 x 7.6 cm), and cut out the floral door panel to be 4¾ x 4 inches (12 x 10.2 cm).

4 Sew the window to a 3-inch (7.6 cm) strip of the house fabric, and then sew on the recipe card, end to end. Next, sew the photo to a 4¾-inch-long (12 cm) strip of house fabric, and seam the door's floral panel patch to the photo and strip of fabric. Press open all the seams. You should have two strips of patches.

5 Sew the panel with the recipe card to the top of a

7¼-inch (18.4 cm) length of the house fabric strips you cut out earlier. Then sew the photo panel to the bottom, and press open the seams.

6 Cut out a triangle of fabric 6 x 6 x 7¼ inches (15.2 x 15.2 x 18.4 cm). Sew a 1-inch-wide (2.5 cm) roof strip to the right 6-inch (15.2 cm) side of the triangle. Sew the other roof strip to the left 6-inch (15.2) side of the triangle, and make sure to overlap the other roof strip as well. Sew the roof to the top of the finished patchwork house.

7 Use the house as a template to cut a back panel and two pieces of batting trimmed a ¼ inch (0.6 cm) smaller than the house. Pin together right sides fac-

OUTER SPACE

Printable cotton sheets are available at many quilting and craft stores. You can use the extra cotton to print pictures for other projects, but be sure to leave unused ½-inch (1.3 cm) portions between photos for the seam allowance.

ing with a short piece of bias tape across the peak of the roof, with the tape sandwiched between the layers to act as a hanging loop on the back.

8 Seam the patchwork to the backing, and leave a 5-inch (12.7 cm) opening on the bottom. Trim the corners, and turn it inside out. Insert the batting into the opening at the bottom.

9 From the roof fabric, cut out the 2 x 3-inch (5.1 x 7.6 cm) door. Press under all sides, and pin

IN THE SPOTLIGHT

You may choose to hand appliqué the door into place then stitch to highlight the house and aspects of the photo. For freehand stitches, try using tailor's chalk and a ruler to mark lines to follow.

in place on the flowered patch. Using a hidden stitch (see page 22), close up the opening at the bottom, tucking in the door bottom. With a doubled black thread, do freehand quilting. Stitch the button in the roof area.

granny's
not square

Give Grandma a makeover with crocheted lace doilies sewn on colorful contemporary fabric. The look is sweet and old-fashioned, but with a youthful twist.

DESIGNER

JOAN K. MORRIS

WHAT YOU NEED

Basic Potholder Tool Kit (page 11)

10 x 20-inch (25.4 x 50.8 cm) piece large floral cotton fabric

10 x 20-inch (25.4 x 50.8 cm) piece light color felt

5 x 10-inch (12.7 x 25.4 cm) piece of pink, striped cotton fabric

10 x 10-inch piece (25.4 x 25.4 cm) of quilt batting

6-inch-round (15.2 cm) piece of crocheted lace

Matching thread

Invisible thread

5 inches (12.7 cm) of ½-inch (1.3 cm) yellow ribbon

WHAT YOU DO

1 Using a plate or other item 9 inches (22.9 cm) around, draw a circle on scrap paper, and cut it out to make the pattern. Fold the floral fabric in half to create a doubled 10-inch (25.4 cm) square. Pin the pattern in place on the folded fabric, and cut out the fabric.

2 With the round pattern, cut out two pieces of felt and one piece of the quilt batting. Cut the striped fabric in half to create two 5 x 5-inch (12.7 x 12.7 cm) pieces of fabric.

3 Place the striped pieces of fabric right sides together, and machine stitch ½ inch (1.3 cm) in from the edge, leaving a 3-inch (7.6 cm) opening on one side. Clip the corners (see page 18), and turn the square right side out. Press the square flat with the opening folded inside. Hand stitch the opening closed.

4 Cut the center flower out of the crocheted lace piece. Machine stitch the flower in place in the center of the striped square using invisible thread in the top,

and regular thread in the bobbin. Stitch around the outside edge of the flower and around the center.

5 Place one of the felt circles on the back side of one of the floral circles. Layer the quilt batting and then another piece of felt under the first piece of felt. Machine baste around the edge of the circles close to the edge.

6 Using the striped square as a guide, place the outside part of the crocheted piece in position in the center of the floral circle. Machine stitch the piece in place using invisible thread in the top, and regular thread in the bobbin. Stitch around the outside edge and the inside edge.

7 Place the striped square in the center of the floral circle, and stitch in place using the matching thread. Decide where to place the ribbon holder. Fold the ribbon in half, and baste it in position, with the folded portion lying to the inside of the circle and the raw edges at the edge.

8 Place and pin the last circle of the floral fabric right sides together with the layered piece. Machine stitch around the edge ½ inch (1.3 cm) in from the edge all the way around, and leave a 3-inch (7.6 cm) opening. Make small clips all the way around, and be careful not to clip into the seam.

9 Press the edges flat. Fold and press the open section as well. Hand stitch the opening closed, and hide your stitches. Topstitch all the way around the edge ½ inch (1.3 cm) in from the edge.

HOOKING UP

Craft stores sell small doilies, but it's a lot more fun to rummage around for granny squares and lace in antique malls or thrift stores. Be on the lookout for bagged lots of random textile bits.

*girly*garden

How does this garden grow? With appliquéd daisies, French-knotted daffodils, and beaded lilies, all in a row.

DESIGNER

JOAN K. MORRIS

WHAT YOU NEED

Basic Potholder Tool Kit (page 11)

12 x 12-inch (30.5 x 30.5 cm) square of green, purple, and blue cotton print

9 x 9-inch (22.9 x 22.9 cm) piece of green corduroy

2 pieces of felt, each 9 x 9 inches (22.9 x 22.9 cm)

2 pieces of green corduroy, 5½ x 7 inches (14 x 17.8 cm)

Assorted purple, pink, and orange cotton prints, each 3 x 3 inches (7.6 x 7.6 cm)

6 inches (15.2 cm) of light green rickrack, ½ inch (1.3 cm) wide

Matching green thread

Knitting needle

Iron-on adhesive

4 inches (10.2 cm) of pink plaid ribbon, ⅛ inch wide (0.3 cm)

4 inches (10.2 cm) of dark green rickrack, ⅛ inch (0.3 cm) wide

Invisible thread

Pink button

Green glass bead

Pink glass bead

Pink, purple, orange, and blue embroidery floss

Embroidery needle

WHAT YOU DO

1 Using scrap paper, make a 9-inch-square (22.9 x 22.9 cm) pattern. (Your piece will be 8 inches [20.3 cm] square after sewing.) Pin the pattern to the piece of green, purple, and blue cotton fabric on a diagonal, and cut it out. Cut out a piece of the 9 x 9-inch (22.9 x 22.9 cm) green corduroy and two pieces of felt the same size.

2 At one corner of the green, purple, and blue fabric, place the piece of light green rickrack, folded in half, for the handle. Place the fold toward the center and the raw edges into the corner. Baste in position.

3 Place the felt pieces under the wrong side of the green, purple, and blue fabric. Place the green corduroy right sides together with the green, purple, and blue fabric. Machine stitch all the way around the edge, ½ inch (1.3 cm) in from the edge. Leave a 3-inch (7.6 cm) opening on one edge. Clip the corners (see page 18).

4 Turn the piece right sides out. Push out the corners with the knitting needle. Press. Press the open section folded in. Hand stitch closed. Machine topstitch all around the edge ½ inch (1.3 cm) in from the edge.

5 Place the 5½ x 7-inch (14 x 17.8 cm) pieces of corduroy right sides together. (You will have a 4½ x 6-inch [11.4 x 15.2 cm] piece after sewing.) Machine stitch all around the edge ½ inch (1.3 cm) in, and leave a 3-inch (7.6 cm) opening on one edge. Clip the corners.

6 Turn the piece right sides out, and push out the corners with the knitting needle. Press with the opening folded to the inside. Hand stitch closed.

7 Following the manufacturer's instructions for the iron-on adhesive, place the adhesive on the back of the three floral prints. Draw the flower designs on the paper backing of the adhesive, and cut out the flowers.

8 Place the flowers on the corduroy, and pin them down (figure 1). Pin the ribbon and rickrack on so they look like stems. Remove the flowers. Zigzag the ribbon and rickrack in place using invisible thread in the needle and regular thread in the bobbin.

figure 1

9 Remove the paper backing from the flowers, and press in place on the corduroy piece. Zigzag, with invisible thread in the needle, around the whole edge of each flower, and make sure the needle hits the flower and the corduroy. Make the stitches close together.

10 Hand stitch the buttons and beads in position on the flowers. Embellish the flowers with embroidery floss. Use a straight stitch and French knots (see page 22). Attach the corduroy piece, and use the blue embroidery thread with a blanket stitch all the way around the edge.

STICKY SITUATION

Because you're drawing on the paper backing of the iron-on adhesive, keep in mind the finished appliqué will be the reverse of any pattern you use.

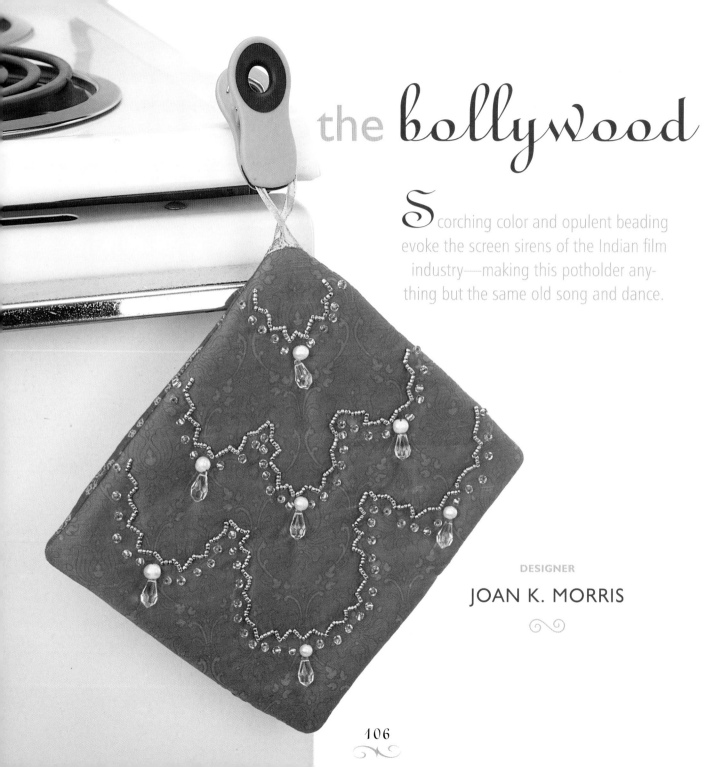

the **bollywood**

Scorching color and opulent beading evoke the screen sirens of the Indian film industry—making this potholder anything but the same old song and dance.

DESIGNER

JOAN K. MORRIS

WHAT YOU NEED

Basic Potholder Tool Kit (page 11)

9 x 9-inch (22.9 x 22.9 cm) piece of pink printed silk

9 x 9-inch (22.9 x 22.9 cm) piece of pink printed cotton

2 pieces of felt, each 9 x 9 inches (22.9 x 22.9 cm)

9 x 9-inch (22.9 x 22.9 cm) piece of quilt batting

Beading needle

Matching thread

7 pearl beads, 8 mm

1 package of E-size clear glass beads

1 package of gold glass seed beads

7 crystal drop beads, 1/8-inch (1.6 cm)

6 inches (15.2 cm) of gold mesh ribbon, 3/8-inches (1 cm) wide

Knitting needle

WHAT YOU DO

1 Make a 9 x 9-inch (22.9 x 22.9 cm) pattern from scrap paper. Using the pattern, cut a piece of the silk, a piece of the cotton, a piece of the quilt batting, and two pieces of felt.

2 Machine baste close to the edge all the way around the piece of silk, face up, with a piece of felt underneath to make it easier to bead the silk.

3 On the pattern piece, draw the layout of where you'll place the beads on the silk. Measure in 3/4 inch (1.9 cm) from the edge all the way around to keep the beading away from the stitching.

4 Transfer the design onto the silk by marking points with a water-soluble marker of where to place the pearl beads first. Stitch the pearls in place using the beading needle and doubled matching thread. Run the thread through twice, and knot it in the back.

5 With the marker, draw the curved lines from pearl to pearl, and stitch the clear glass beads in position.

6 Above the clear glass beads, stitch on the gold seed beads four at a time in a zigzag. Knot the thread on the back side every other set of four beads. Under each pearl, stitch on each crystal drop bead, running the thread through twice. Machine baste the second piece of felt behind the first, over the same stitch line as the first.

7 Place the gold ribbon folded in half at the top corner of the front of the beaded silk piece with the raw edges up. Machine baste in place.

8 Place the cotton piece right sides together with the silk piece, and pin in place. Machine stitch around the edge 1/2 inch (1.3 cm) in from the edge, and leave a 3-inch (7.6 cm) opening along one lower edge.

9 Clip the corners (see page 18), and turn right sides out, then push the corners out with the knitting needle. Press the whole thing flat with the opening folded in place. Hand stitch the opening closed, and hide the stitches.

*sew*romantic

As every domestic goddess knows, it's all about presentation. Dress up your dish with this pin-tucked potholder, and the simplest meal will feel like a romantic dinner.

DESIGNER

VALERIE SHRADER

WHAT YOU NEED

Basic Potholder Tool Kit (page 11)

Fabric scraps for decoration

¼ yard (22.9 cm) of lightweight fabric for the front

¼ yard (22.9 cm) of medium-weight fabric for the back

2 pieces of craft felt, each 9 x 12 inches (22.9 x 30.5 cm)

Rotary cutter

Cutting mat

Pin-tucking foot (optional)

Point turner (optional)

SEAM ALLOWANCE

¼ inch (0.6 cm)

WHAT YOU DO

1 Cut about a yard (0.9 m) of ½-inch (1.3 cm) strips from the fabric scraps for decoration and for the hanger. Cut a 9-inch (22.9 cm) square from the lightweight fabric and the medium-weight fabric.

2 Using the pin-tucking foot and beginning ⅝ inch (1.6 cm) from the edge of the lightweight piece, stitch a series of eight or 10 pin tucks. Skip about ⅝ inch (1.6 cm), and make another pin tuck, this time stitching on a decorative strip as you sew. Continue in this fashion as desired, alternating decorated tucks with groupings of plain tucks.

3 Because the pin tucking may distort the shape of the potholder front, trim it to 8 x 8 inches (20.3 x 20.3 cm), squaring it up. Cut two pieces of craft felt of that size, too.

4 Use the leftover decorative strips to make the hanger. Take two strips, and stitch them together with the wrong sides facing, continuing to use the pin-tucking foot. Trim it to about 6 inches (15.2 cm).

5 Cut enough 1-inch (2.5 cm) bias strips to fit around the circumference of your potholder plus at least 1 additional inch (2.5 cm), interspersing the various fabrics as desired. (You should have a minimum of 32 inches [81.3 cm].) Stitch the strips together to make bias tape (see page 20). Press under ½ inch (1.3 cm) on one long edge of the bias tape.

6 Make a sandwich: place the back of the potholder with the wrong side facing up; add two layers of felt; then place the front of the potholder on top with the right side facing up. Fold the hanger, and place it in the desired corner on the front, with the raw edges slightly extending past the raw edges of the potholder. Baste the hanger in place.

7 Fold under one short edge of the binding. Pin the binding to the front of the potholder, right sides facing. Sew it down, mitering the corners (see page 21).

8 Trim the seam to ⅛ inch (0.3 cm). Turn the binding to the wrong side and press; the folded edge should cover the seam line. Slipstitch in place (see page 22).

TUCKED IN

If you don't have a pin-tucking foot, you can mark and stitch narrow folds along the length of your fabric to replicate this look.

kitchenette

silhouette

DESIGNER

JOAN K. MORRIS

*P*retty as a picture, the flower silhouettes of these sturdy potholders will look great hanging on the wall in between use. Find clip art of your favorite flowers, and use iron-on transfers to complete the look.

WHAT YOU NEED

Basic Potholder Tool Kit (page 11)

¼ yard (22.9 cm) floral cotton fabric

¼ yard (22.9 cm) striped cotton fabric

4 pieces of felt, 7 x 9½ inches (17.8 x 24.1 cm)

Clip art silhouette flower designs

2 iron-on transfer sheets for inkjet printers, each 8½ x 11 inches (21.6 x 27.9 cm)

Computer

Printer

2 pieces of quilt batting, 7 x 9½ inches (17.8 x 24.1 cm)

Matching thread

12 inches (30.5 cm) of matching cord

WHAT YOU DO

1 Cut out a piece of the floral fabric and a piece of the striped fabric 6 x 10 inches (15.2 x 25.4 cm). Select clip art silhouettes of flower designs.

2 Following the manufacturer's instructions for the iron-on transfer paper, print out two flower designs onto the transfer paper. Cut around the designs then iron them onto the right sides of the cut-out fabric pieces (figure 1).

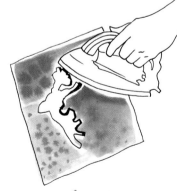

figure 1

3 Create a pattern by cutting a piece of scrap paper 7 x 9½ inches (17.8 x 24.1 cm). Use it to cut out two pieces of the floral fabric, two pieces of the striped fabric, four pieces of the felt, and two pieces of the quilt batting.

4 Cut the cord into two 6-inch (15.2 cm) pieces. Place one piece at the top center of one of the 7 x 9½-inch (17.8 x 24.1 cm) pieces of the floral fabric and one of the striped pieces. Fold the cord in half with the raw edge lined up with the raw edge of the fabric. Machine baste the cords in place ¼ inch (0.6 cm) in from the edge.

5 Under the fabric pieces with the cord, layer a piece of felt, then a layer of quilt batting, and then another piece of felt. Place the matching piece of fabric right sides together with the first piece. Machine stitch around the edge ½ inch (1.3 cm) in from the edge, and leave a 3-inch (7.6 cm) opening at the bottom. Clip the corners (see page 18).

6 Turn the piece right sides out through the 3-inch (7.6 cm) opening. Iron flat, and fold the opening closed, then hand stitch it shut, hiding the stitches. Take the two pieces of fabric with the iron-on flowers, and fold the edges under to create 3 x 6-inch (7.6 x 15.2 cm) pieces. Leave the extra fabric under the pieces.

7 Center the striped piece with the flower on the floral piece, and pin in place. Center the floral piece with the flower on the striped fabric piece, and pin it in place.

8 Set the machine to a long stitch length—but not one for basting—and sew all the way around the edge of the flower piece.

9 Using the same long stitch, sew all the way around the outside, ½ inch (1.3 cm) from the edge.

DISTENTION PREVENTION

To keep the fabric from stretching, it's best to stitch across the top first, then down one side, and then start at the top and down the other side; finally, stitch across the bottom.

butterfly flutter

Rickrack antennae and button embellishments make this potholder pop, but the real wow factor is the pocket formed by the double-layered wings. Simply slip your fingers in, and watch this butterfly flutter like the real thing.

DESIGNER

LAURRAINE YUYAMA

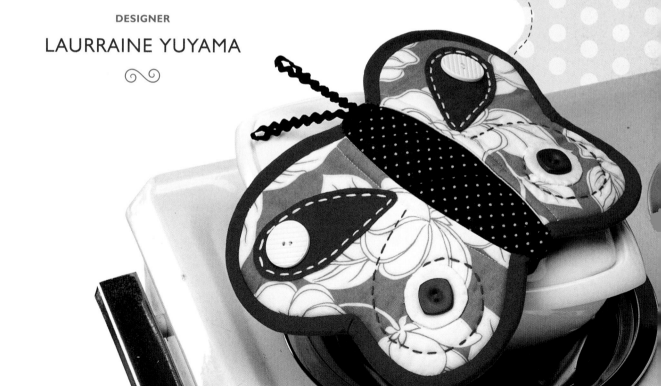

WHAT YOU NEED

Basic Potholder Tool Kit (page 11)

¼ yard (22.9 cm) of fabric for the body

6 inches (15.2 cm) of fabric for the wings

Fat quarter of fabric for the binding and the wing appliqués

Small scraps of fabric for the wing appliqués

Rotary cutter and mat (optional)

Rickrack

¼ yard (22.9 cm) of heat-repellent oven mitt batting

White thread

Black thread

Chopstick or knitting needle

Embroidery needle

Purple embroidery floss

White embroidery floss

2 white buttons, each 1⅛ inches (2.8 cm) in diameter

2 purple buttons, each ¾ inch (1.9 cm) in diameter

SEAM ALLOWANCE

⅜ inch (1 cm)

WHAT YOU DO

CUT

1 Enlarge the templates on page 120, cut them out, and use them as patterns to cut out the fabric pieces. Cut out one front body on the fold, as instructed on the template. Cut two wings out of the fabric that will show—one with the pattern piece facing up and one with it facing down—and two wings out of lining material.

2 For the back, cut a rectangle 9 x 12 inches (22.9 x 30.5 cm). From the same fabric, cut two squares on the bias, each 2 x 2 inches (5.1 x 5.1 cm), to use as binding (see page 20).

3 Cut the fat quarter in half diagonally. Cut strips 2 inches (5.1 cm) wide on either side of the cut, so you end up with two bias strips 2 x 15½ inches (5.1 x 39.4 cm). From the same fabric, cut four of the upper wing appliqués.

4 Cut four of the lower wing appliqués.

5 From the rickrack, cut two pieces 8 inches (20.3 cm) long.

6 From the batting, cut two rectangles, each 9 x 12 inches (22.9 x 30.5 cm), and two others, each 6 x 9 inches (15.2 x 22.9 cm).

ASSEMBLE

1 Lay the back rectangle right side down; place two layers of the larger rectangles of batting over it, and then place the front body right side up on top. Quilt the stack by sewing a diagonal grid with lines 1½ inches (3.8 cm) apart through all four layers (figure 1). Trim the batting.

2 To make the antennae, fold each piece of rickrack in half

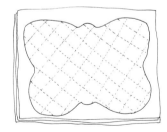

figure 1

and sew along most of the length, leaving an open loop at the end for hanging the potholder. Tack the antennae to the head, with the raw edges matching and the antennae placed across the body.

3 Bind the head and tail of the butterfly by folding the bias squares 1/4 inch (0.6 cm) in on the sides. Pin to the front of the body, right sides together and aligning the edges, and stitch. Flip the binding over to the back, and tuck in the corners. Fold the binding under 3/8 inch (1 cm), and whipstitch it to the back side.

4 Match each wing to its lining, placing them right sides together, and pin them to one layer of the remaining batting. Sew along the straighter, inner edge. Trim the batting. Turn right side out, and sew 1/4 inch (0.6 cm) along the same edge.

5 Pair the appliqués so you have two upper ones and two lower ones. Stitch them to each other, right sides together. Trim the seams of each pair to 1/8 inch (0.3 cm). Cut a slit in one face, and turn the appliqués right side out, using the chopstick or knitting needle. Press.

6 Transfer the spiral from the template onto the wings. Using contrasting embroidery floss, sew a heavy straight stitch along the lines. Pin the appliqué pieces to the wing and stitch them on, 1/8 inch (0.3 cm) from the edge, using a heavy straight stitch in contrasting embroidery floss. Attach the buttons.

7 Pin the wings to the body, keeping the pins away from the edges. Fold the bias strips in 1/4 inch (0.6 cm) at the ends, and pin them along the outer edge of the wings. Sew all the layers together, folding and trimming any excess bias strip when you get to the end of the wing. Fold the strip over to the back, fold the corners, and whipstitch in place. Use a few stitches to secure ends of the binding. Fold the antennae to point up as they do in nature, and tack them so they remain that way.

TAKING WING

Aligning the wings and the front body will help with positioning the appliqué shapes.

pompoms and pearls

$\mathcal{T}$he pearls may be faux, but with playful pompoms
and a flirty print, this pair of potholders is 100% pure fun!

DESIGNER
VALERIE SHRADER

WHAT YOU NEED

Basic Potholder Tool Kit (page 11)

1/4 yard (22.9 cm) each of
2 different fabrics

3 pieces of craft felt (to line the
pocket and provide insulation),
9 x 12 inches (22.9 x 30.5 cm)
each

Rotary cutter

Cutting mat

1 skein variegated embroidery
floss, in color to match fabrics

Hand-embroidery needles

Faux pearls

Invisible thread

Point turner (optional)

Pompoms to match fabrics

SEAM ALLOWANCE

1/2 inch (1.3 cm)

WHAT YOU DO

1 For the main body of the potholder, cut a square of fabric 9 x 9 inches (22.9 x 22.9 cm). For the pocket and the back, cut two squares from the remaining fabric, each also 9 x 9 inches (22.9 x 22.9 cm).

2 Fold the pocket piece in half diagonally, and mark the top if necessary. Using the folded piece as a guide, cut a piece of craft felt to this triangular shape, trimming away the seam allowance on the two shorter edges. Unfold the pocket. Pin the felt triangle to the wrong side of the top of the pocket, centering it between the seam allowances. (This lining will provide heat protection and help stabilize the embroidery you'll do in the next step.)

3 Using the stitches of your choice (see page 22–23), embroider the top of the pocket to highlight some of the motifs on the fabric. Add the faux pearls as desired with the invisible thread.

4 After you've finished embroidering, fold the undecorated part of the flap over the felt triangle (figure 1). Baste the pocket to the main body of the potholder.

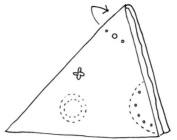

figure 1

5 With the right sides together, pin and stitch the back of the potholder to the decorated front, leaving one side open to turn. Trim the seam allowances.

6 Turn the potholder right side out through the opening, and use the point turner as necessary to sharpen the corners. Cut two pieces of craft felt to fit inside the potholder. Stitch them together, and then slip them inside the potholder.

7 Press the opening closed and slipstitch together. Add the pompoms to accent the potholder as desired, using a matching color of thread.

templates

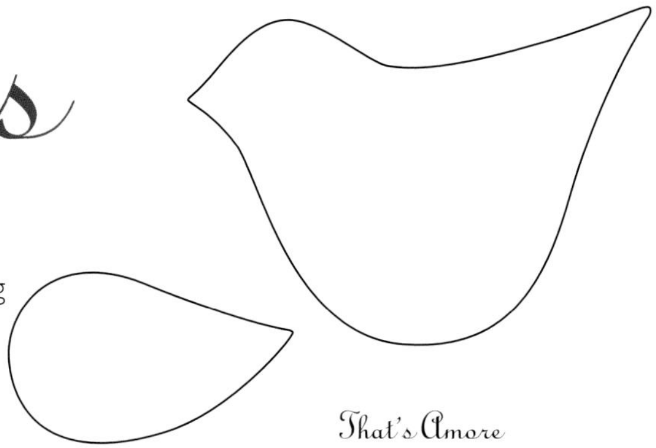

Wing

That's Amore

Page 78

Enlarge 150%

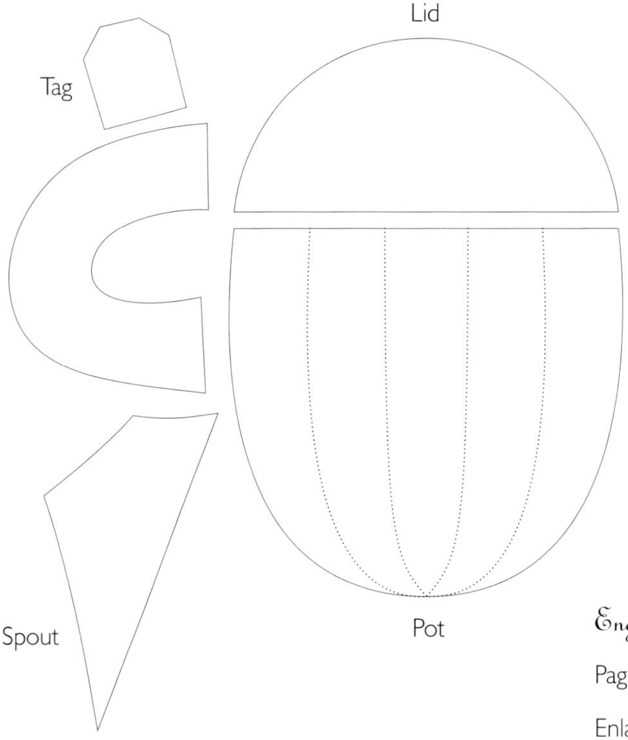

Tag

Lid

Handle

Spout

Pot

English Breakfast

Page 84

Enlarge 400%

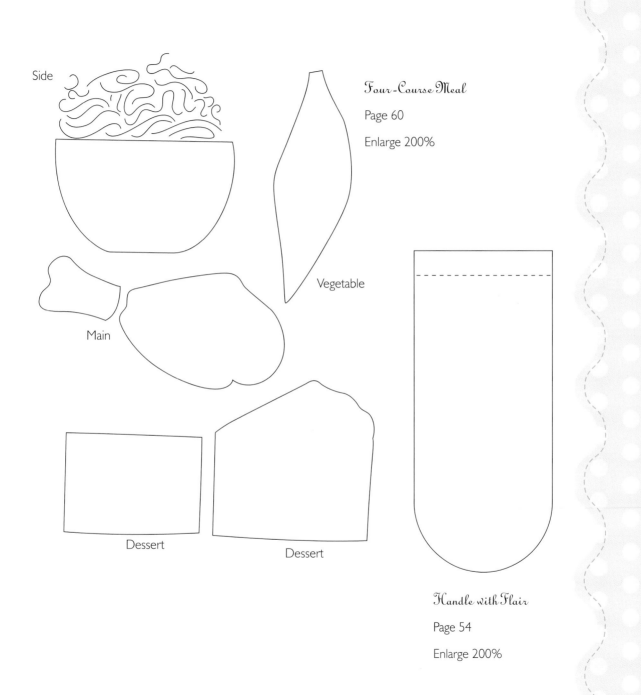

Side

Four-Course Meal

Page 60

Enlarge 200%

Vegetable

Main

Dessert

Dessert

Handle with Flair

Page 54

Enlarge 200%

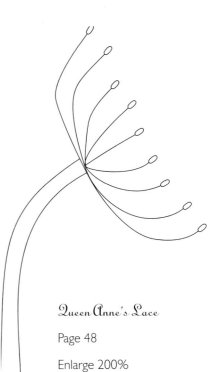

Lovely Lotus

Page 87

Enlarge 200%

Queen Anne's Lace

Page 48

Enlarge 200%

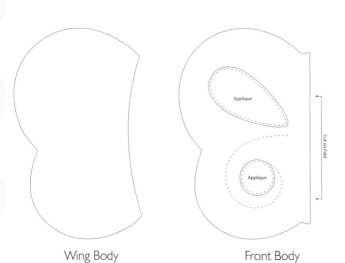

Applique

Applique

Cut on Fold

Butterfly Flutter

Page 113

Enlarge 400%

Wing Body

Front Body

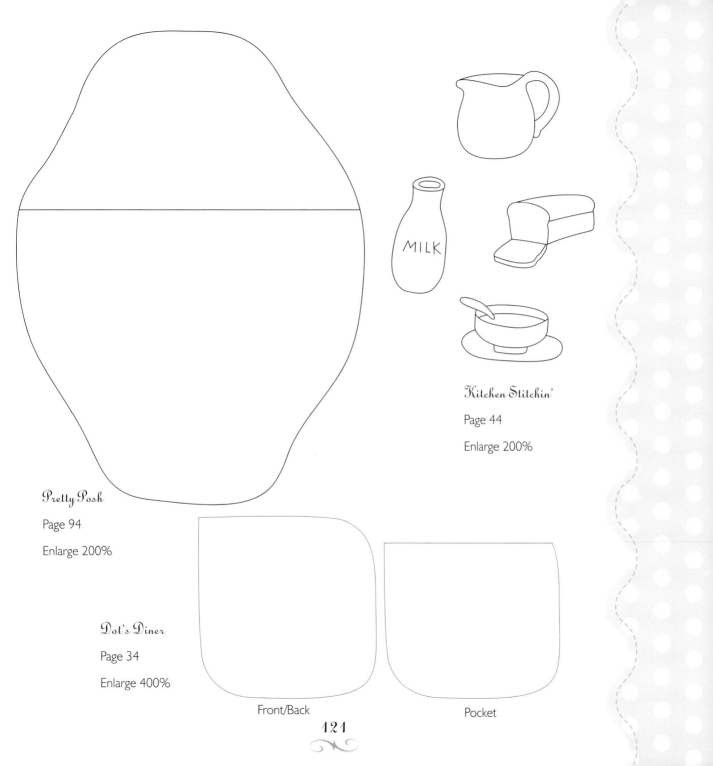

Pretty Posh
Page 94
Enlarge 200%

Kitchen Stitchin'
Page 44
Enlarge 200%

Dot's Diner
Page 34
Enlarge 400%

Front/Back

Pocket

Sweet Treat

Page 46

Enlarge 200%

Salsa Softies

Page 28

Enlarge 400%

Scorchin'!

Page 57

Enlarge 300%

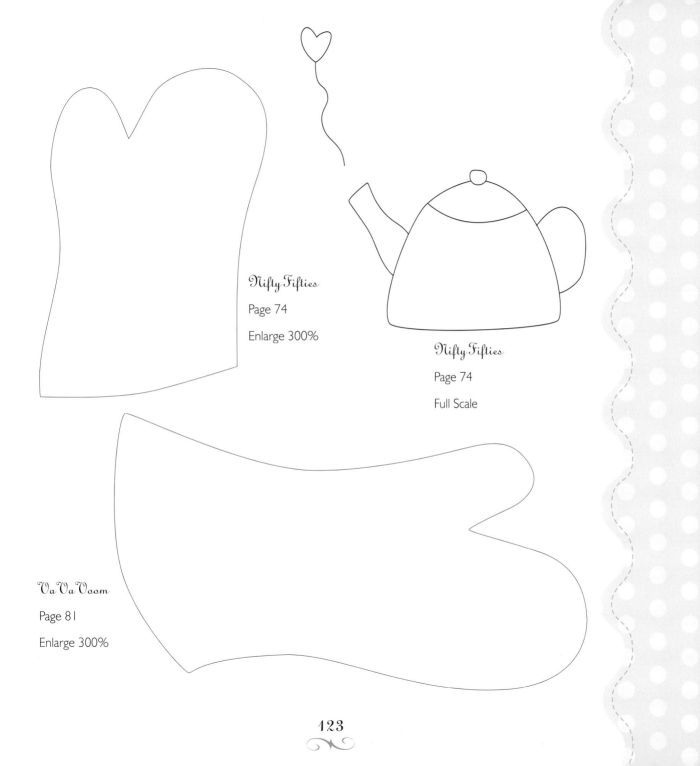

Nifty Fifties

Page 74

Enlarge 300%

Nifty Fifties

Page 74

Full Scale

Va Va Voom

Page 81

Enlarge 300%

about the designers

ELEANORE BOCKHEIM has been a women's clothing designer, a radio and television show host, a weaver, a quilter and sewer, and an international needlework teacher. She has written five in-depth study workbooks on open-weave needlework techniques. Eleanore is now retired and lives in Grandville, Michigan.

BETSY COUZINS has been working as a mixed-media artist ever since her pilgrim diorama received an A in the second grade. Her work has been featured in *Altered Art* (Lark, 2004) and *The Decorated Journal* (Lark, 2005), as well as in several national periodicals including *Jane* and *Artitude*. She currently resides in Asheville, North Carolina, with her husband and son. Her blog, located at http://wonderland5.typepad.com, chronicles her increasing love of working with fabric.

MAITREYA DUNHAM is a scientist and teacher by day, and a crafter by night. She posts the latest sewing, embroidery, crochet, and other craft projects she's got cooking at craftlog.org, which has been running since 2003. Her creative influences include Japanese craft books and the ever-growing number of craft blogs on the Internet. She is lucky enough to have a group of friends, all scientists, who meet up for regular craft nights to sew, knit, and trade lab gossip. A previously published crafter, Maitreya is also a contributor to the collaborative craft blog Whip Up at whipup.net. In addition, she maintains a site devoted to Japanese craft books—found at craftlog.org/craftingjapanese—and a searchable index of favorite magazine articles. She lives in New Jersey with her husband, Mark, and two cats, Becket and el Chupacabra.

LIESL GIBSON tries to keep herself out of trouble by simultaneously chasing a busy toddler, maintaining her blog at http://disdressed.blogspot.com, teaching sewing at Purl Patchwork in New York City, and designing patterns for children's clothing. She has been up past bedtime virtually every night since 2005. Liesl lives in Manhattan. She and her grandmother, Eleanore Bockheim, collaborated on the project in this book.

WENDI GRATZ lives in Bakersville, North Carolina, with her family and her sewing machine. At school, she skipped Home Ec in favor of wood and metal shop and didn't learn to use a sewing machine until she was in college. Her first project was a badly made tablecloth. She learned a lot from that disastrous project. Her second venture was designing and making all the costumes for a play. Now she makes fun clothes, funky dolls, and all kinds of quilts. You can see her work at www.wendigratz.com and in other Lark titles, including *Simple Contemporary Quilts* (2006).

AUTUM HALL lives in North Carolina with her husband, two children, and too many pets to name. Despite being raised by an accomplished seamstress, she initially resisted the needle and thread. In her thirties, she took up sewing as a way to decorate on a budget. She began by sewing curtains and pillows for her home. It wasn't long before her daughter started requesting handbags, and the demand just took off. Daisy Goods began as a small business designing unique handbags and home décor for local folks. Now, thanks to the Internet, her wares sell all over the world. For more information, visit www.daisygoods.com.

REBEKA LAMBERT lives with her husband and three small children on the outskirts of Baton Rouge, Louisiana. She received her bachelor's degree in liberal arts with a concentration in art history from Louisiana State University in 1997. Rebeka works in the IT field, though she hopes to one day fulfill her dream of creating and designing full time. When she isn't working or spending time with her family, she enjoys creating projects in her sewing studio. Her favorite things to make are bags and purses. Though she has crafted for most of her life, her love of sewing began as a child by watching her mother and grandmother sew. She is a self-proclaimed fabric addict. Her passion for textiles developed in college while working at a fabric store. After putting crafting on hold during her early years of motherhood, Rebeka is back, in full force. It was the discovery of blogs, particularly craft blogs, which led her back to crafting, and it is the daily feedback and sharing of ideas through blogging that keeps her inspired. Catch a glimpse of her life on her blog, http://artsycraftybabe.typepad.com.

BETHANY MANN is a crafty mom who resides in the Santa Cruz mountains with her husband, son, and a couple of cats. A former window dresser and file clerk, Bethany is currently obsessed with sewing clothes from vintage patterns, jewelry making, and gardening. When she isn't home—trying to keep the deer out of the yard or begging the tree peony to bloom already—she spends her time in thrift stores and flea markets looking for raw crafting materials and colorful anecdotes for her blog, bitterbettyindustries.blogspot.com.

SARAH MCDOUGALL has loved arts and crafts ever since she won the annual Christmas window-painting display contest in second grade. Not only does she have a passion for vintage fabrics, but she also bakes tasty treats, crochets blankets, and scours the Internet for the latest creative craft blogs. Sarah received her bachelor's degree in photography from Arizona State University in 2004. While in college she made her friend take a fibers course with her. Her friend hated the class, but Sarah fell in love and has had a fabric obsession ever since. She currently resides in Arizona with her Chihuahua, Chico; her cat, Caesar; and the goldfish, Oscar. More of her potholders and various handmade items can be found at www.anappealtoheaven.etsy.com.

NATHALIE MORNU works as an editor at Lark Books. She occasionally gets to design projects for books, which gives her a chance to dabble at various crafts. Her projects appear in numerous titles published by Lark, among them *Decorating Your First Apartment* (2003), *Making Gingerbread Houses* (2004), and *Pretty Little Pincushions* (2007). She's the co-author of *Contemporary Bead & Wire Jewelry* (2006) and *Survival Sewing* (2007), and the author of *Cutting-Edge Decoupage* (2007), also published by Lark. Nathalie is currently fixated on embroidery.

JOAN K. MORRIS'S artistic endeavors have led her down many successful creative paths, including ceramics and costume design for motion pictures. Joan has contributed projects to numer-ous Lark books, including *Cutting Edge Decoupage* (2007), *Creative Stitching on Paper* (2006), *Exquisite Embellishments for Your Clothes* (2006), *Beautiful Ribbon Crafts* (2003), *Gifts For Baby* (2004), *Hardware Style* (2004), and *Hip Handbags* (2005).

AIMEE RAY has been making things for as long as she can remember, and has a head full of ideas. As a graphic designer in the greeting card and comic book industries—and with several personal projects in the works—she is never without something creative in hand. Her interests range from digital painting and illustration to sewing stuffed animals, embroidery, and everything else in between. She is the author of *Doodle Stitching* (Lark, 2007), a book of contemporary embroidery designs and projects. You can see more of Aimee's work at her website, www.dreamfollow.com.

CHRISTINA ROMEO is a multimedia artist with a strong pull toward textile design. As a child, she learned to cross-stitch, collage, and reconstruct clothes into abstract creations. After a 10-year career in the dental health profes-sion, Christina now pursues art full time, selling work throughout Canada and the United States. Her work appears in the Lark books *Simple Contemporary Quilts* (2007) and *Quilting with Beads* (2008). Her studio is located in the heart of the Selkirk Mountains in Revelstoke, British Columbia. For more information, visit www.jamtartbaby.com.

DORIE BLAISDELL SCHWARZ has been wielding a needle and thread and designing in notebook margins since second grade. A Jersey Shore native, she now lives in a small town called Farmer City with her husband and her daughter. When she's not sewing, Dorie builds websites, helps renovate her home, and enjoys the company of friends and family. She keeps a craft blog about her love of making things at tumblingblocks.net/blog/.

VALERIE SHRADER made a pair of pink culottes when she was 11 and has loved fabric ever since. Recently, she celebrated her midlife crisis by purchasing three sewing machines in one year. Valerie is on the staff of Lark Books and has written and edited many books related to textiles and needlework. She knits every now and then, too, and hopes that art quilts will be her next creative exploration.

SHANNON UDELL designs funky little fabric patches, dolls, art quilts, and other goodies from her home in California, and sells them from her online store, Mukibubb Folklore Boutique at mukibubb. etsy.com. She grew up in the 1970s in small-town Sacramento and is the daughter of a textile artist mother and a photographer father. Her love and vision for art and all things handmade grew quietly in a hideaway beneath a large oval quilting frame with her very own needle and scraps. The blocky forms in her work are inspired by the homespun items that she wore as a child and by the earliest artwork of her children. Shannon shares her creative home with her husband, Scott, crafty daughters, Megan and Brigit, and their two lazy dogs. When she's not sewing, she's in her garden, reading a book, or attending a church function.

JENNIFER WALLIN may spend her days toiling away at her 9 to 5 job, but crafting is always on her mind. Once she gets home at night to join her husband, dog, and two cats in Long Beach, California, Jennifer tries to cram in a little crafting to balance the grind of working in an uncreative field. She has participated in monthly craft-a-longs to create aprons, potholders, and purses. See more of her work at thefeltmouse.blogspot.com.

KAREN WITTKOP got her first children's sewing machine when she was five years old and became the proud owner of her first real machine by the age of twelve. Needless to say, she had the best-dressed dolls around! As a stay-at-home mom, she looked to sewing and crafting to help maintain her sanity. Now, with her children grown, she's turned her hobby into a business. Karen recently opened up shop online and sells her wares at misseskwittys. etsy.com. She's astounded by the colorful, delicate, and painstaking embellishments found on vintage dish towels, doilies, hankies, and other everyday objects. Her work honors the women who came before her—women who made everything from scratch and took the time to make it all painstakingly beautiful.

LAURRAINE YUYAMA used to work as a custom picture framer but found herself wanting to create her own art instead. She left the glass cutters and frames behind and now spends her days surrounded with beautiful fabric, buttons, ribbons, and clay. In the last five years, she discovered a passion for fabric and clay and has developed a style of surface designs that she uses with both pottery and quilted items. Her work combines beautiful patterns from nature with unique functional items such as bags and bowls. Laurraine is a self-taught quilter, and she creates all of her own designs and patterns. She takes inspiration from new fabric, buttons, Japanese craft books, and the Internet craft community. When she's not crafting, she spends time with her little girl and husband. Her work is sold internationally from her home-based studio in Vancouver, Canada, and through her online shop, which you can find at www.patchworkpottery.com.

many books related to textiles and needlework. She knits every now and then, too, and hopes that art quilts will be her next creative exploration.

SHANNON UDELL designs funky little fabric patches, dolls, art quilts, and other goodies from her home in California, and sells them from her online store, Mukibubb Folklore Boutique at mukibubb. etsy.com. She grew up in the 1970s in small-town Sacramento and is the daughter of a textile artist mother and a photographer father. Her love and vision for art and all things handmade grew quietly in a hideaway beneath a large oval quilting frame with her very own needle and scraps. The blocky forms in her work are inspired by the homespun items that she wore as a child and by the earliest artwork of her children. Shannon shares her creative home with her husband, Scott, crafty daughters, Megan and Brigit, and their two lazy dogs. When she's not sewing, she's in her garden, reading a book, or attending a church function.

JENNIFER WALLIN may spend her days toiling away at her 9 to 5 job, but crafting is always on her mind. Once she gets home at night to join her husband, dog, and two cats in Long Beach, California, Jennifer tries to cram in a little crafting to balance the grind of working in an uncreative field. She has participated in monthly craft-a-longs to create aprons, potholders, and purses. See more of her work at thefeltmouse.blogspot.com.

KAREN WITTKOP got her first children's sewing machine when she was five years old and became the proud owner of her first real machine by the age of twelve. Needless to say, she had the best-dressed dolls around! As a stay-at-home mom, she looked to sewing and crafting to help maintain her sanity. Now, with her children grown, she's turned her hobby into a business. Karen recently opened up shop online and sells her wares at misseskwittys. etsy.com. She's astounded by the colorful, delicate, and painstaking embellishments found on vintage dish towels, doilies, hankies, and other everyday objects. Her work honors the women who came before her—women who made everything from scratch and took the time to make it all painstakingly beautiful.

LAURRAINE YUYAMA used to work as a custom picture framer but found herself wanting to create her own art instead. She left the glass cutters and frames behind and now spends her days surrounded with beautiful fabric, buttons, ribbons, and clay. In the last five years, she discovered a passion for fabric and clay and has developed a style of surface designs that she uses with both pottery and quilted items. Her work combines beautiful patterns from nature with unique functional items such as bags and bowls. Laurraine is a self-taught quilter, and she creates all of her own designs and patterns. She takes inspiration from new fabric, buttons, Japanese craft books, and the Internet craft community. When she's not crafting, she spends time with her little girl and husband. Her work is sold internationally from her home-based studio in Vancouver, Canada, and through her online shop, which you can find at www.patchworkpottery.com.

acknowledgments

Grateful thanks to the editorial team that worked on this book: Jess Clarke, Dawn Dillingham, Kathleen McCafferty, and Nathalie Mornu. The art production team of Jeff Hamilton and Travis Medford kept the project smoothly on track.

Susan McBride's sweet little illustrations are much appreciated for the charm they bring to these pages. Photographer Stewart O'Shields helped the projects shine under the bright lights; thanks to his assistant Megan Cox for modeling with such panache! Megan Kirby's spot-on art direction brings out the personality of each potholder.

Finally, a big round of applause goes out to the designers who created the fabulous potholders in this book. This book wouldn't have come together without your creativity. Thanks for sharing your talents!

index